Praise for *Leading People Through Disasters*

"After many years in the people-side of business, and after having witnessed firsthand the devastation of 9/11, it was clear that the people-side of business was in dire need of an instructional guide for use in times of chaos. This 'how to' action guide is a must-read for all of us who want to be better prepared for the next disaster that may come our way . . . even if it is tomorrow."

— Ann Rhoades, President of PeopleInk, current Director and former Executive Vice President of Jet Blue Airways, and former Vice President People, Southwest Airlines

"Trauma is debilitating. The inevitable, recurring waves of flashbacks and survivor guilt render us less adaptive, resilient, sensitive, and creative— just when we need these capabilities the most. Whether from natural disasters, terrorist attacks, or product recalls, crises haunt us all. McKee and Guthridge have written a marvelous book that takes the old Boy Scout motto, 'Be Prepared,' to new heights. It will help you get ready for and make the best of any crisis. If it has not happened to you, or not recently, get ready—it will, and this book will help."

— Richard E. Boyatzis, Professor of Organizational Behavior, Psychology and Human Resources at Case Western Reserve University and ESADE, co-author of the international bestseller *Primal Leadership* and *Resonant Leadership*

"This book is a great resource. It's the only book I've seen that makes such a compelling case to include the people issues, such as employee communication, in your business continuity planning. Plus, it contains some great, practical ideas that all companies can easily implement."

— Kimberly R. Walsh, Vice President, Communications, Pacific Gas and Electric Company

"In *Leading People Through Disasters,* Kathryn McKee and Liz Guthridge have performed a valuable service to the business and HR community. These experienced and insightful professionals have provided a manual that is rich with concepts, tools, and checklists of how to prepare for and respond to the full range of disasters. By following their guidelines, business and HR professionals can step to the fore to address the difficulties and trauma for customers and employees alike. This book should be read and placed on an accessible portion of the book shelf of every business person and HR professional."

—Wayne Brockbank, Clinical Professor of Business, Ross School of Business at the University of Michigan

"Should disaster strike, is your business prepared to deal with the human side of crises? An excellent place to start is with *Leading People Through Disasters*. Preparing to meet disaster can make all the difference, and here's a practical guide that shows you how."

— Richard W. Beatty, Professor of Human Resource Management, Rutgers University, and Core Faculty Member, University of Michigan, Ross School of Business Executive Education Center

"In normal times, to be successful, organizations require the best human leadership we can provide. In troubled times, as the book *Leading People Through Disasters* explains quite convincingly, there's no margin of error. All leaders—including communication professionals—must make sure they are not insulated or isolated from the situation. They must visibly take charge, get their employees to safety, and communicate clearly, concisely, and frequently. Leadership and communication are often synonymous in normal times, and even more so during disasters. This book makes a great business case for being an involved, caring leader who regularly interprets the implications of what is happening. This is the best way to gain the trust and credibility of employees as well as recover jobs and the company."

— Roger D'Aprix, communication consultant and author of *Communicating for Change*, *Communicating for Productivity*, and *The Face-to-Face Communication Toolkit*

"*Leading People Through Disasters* is a terrific 'how-to' guide for anyone in an organization, especially HR and communications professionals. This book makes the point that you've got to prepare for disasters, even when you don't think you have the bandwidth, and explains why this is well worth your time. The act of preparation will make your organization stronger, more nimble, and more confident to take on all sorts of challenges and opportunities coming your way."

— Steve Umphreys, Senior Vice President of Global Employee Services, salesforce.com

Also visit **www.leadingpeoplethroughdisasters.com**

Leading
People
Through
Disasters

Leading People Through Disasters

An Action Guide: Preparing for and Dealing with the Human Side of Crises

Kathryn McKee, SPHR, and Liz Guthridge

BERRETT-KOEHLER PUBLISHERS, INC.
San Francisco

Berrett-Koehler Publishers, Inc.
235 Montgomery Street, Suite 650
San Francisco, CA 94104-2916
Tel: (415) 288-0260   Fax: (415) 362-2512   www.bkconnection.com

Ordering Information

Quantity sales. Special discounts are available on quantity purchases by corporations, associations, and others. For details, contact the "Special Sales Department" at the Berrett-Koehler address above.

Individual sales. Berrett-Koehler publications are available through most bookstores. They can also be ordered directly from Berrett-Koehler: Tel: (800) 929-2929; Fax: (802) 864-7626; www.bkconnection.com

Orders for college textbook/course adoption use. Please contact Berrett-Koehler: Tel: (800) 929-2929; Fax: (802) 864-7626.

Orders by U.S. trade bookstores and wholesalers. Please contact Publishers Group West, 1700 Fourth Street, Berkeley, CA 94710. Tel: (510) 528-1444; Fax (510) 528-3444.

Berrett-Koehler and the BK logo are registered trademarks of Berrett-Koehler Publishers, Inc.

Printed in the United States of America

Berrett-Koehler books are printed on long-lasting acid-free paper. When it is available, we choose paper that has been manufactured by environmentally responsible processes. These may include using trees grown in sustainable forests, incorporating recycled paper, minimizing chlorine in bleaching, or recycling the energy produced at the paper mill.

Library of Congress Cataloging-in-Publication Data
McKee, Kathryn, 1937-
    Leading people through disasters : an action guide / by Kathryn McKee and Liz Guthridge.
        p. cm.
    Includes bibliographical references and index.
    ISBN-13: 978-1-57675-420-7
    1. Crisis management. 2. Emergency management. 3. Personnel management. 4. Employee assistance programs. I. Guthridge, Liz, 1957- II. Title.

HD49.M384 2006   2006040731
658.4'77--dc22

ISBN-10: 1-57675-420-0; ISBN-13: 978-1-57675-420-7

First Edition
11   10   09   08   07   06   10   9   8   7   6   5   4   3   2   1

To my sons, Grant and Scott McKee.

To my husband, David Matthews.

To all of our friends and work colleagues
who have laughed with us—in good times, trying times,
and all times.

Contents

Foreword

As professionals, we often have to deal with challenging events, people, and scenarios. For the most part, we try to make the best of these situations and do what's right for our organizations, our people, and ourselves. And over the years, many of us have learned valuable lessons: Planning is less painful than procrastination, prevention generally requires less time and resource outlay than intervention, and action is more effective and less costly than reaction.

The extraordinary number of catastrophic events during the first half of this decade has created a more intense focus on disaster planning/preparation and crisis management. We've discovered—some of us the hard way—that getting involved in disaster preparedness is one of the most important contributions we can make to our organizations. And while we hope that disaster never strikes, we've learned to be prepared for the worst at all times. "Chicken Little" notwithstanding, sometimes the sky *really does* fall.

Many members of the Society for Human Resource Management (SHRM) are actively participating in the development and implementation of organizational disaster plans. More than 75% of respondents to the SHRM 2005 Disaster Preparedness Survey[1] claimed to have played some role in their organizations' disaster preparedness plans. However, the survey also revealed that only slightly more than half of the organizations created or revised disaster preparedness plans after the terrorist attacks of September 11, 2001, and 45% did neither. Although the events of September 11 may have begun to fade from recent memory, the rash of natural disasters during the fall of 2005 should remind HR professionals and other business leaders of the critical importance of disaster planning and should motivate them to implement effective crisis management programs.

As HR professionals, however, we need to do more. We need to take to heart the key message in this important book: *Disaster preparedness plans must address the human component.* We must recognize that we depend on people to carry out essential duties when disaster strikes, particularly if we're to continue running our businesses. All too often, disaster preparedness plans focus more on organizational infrastructure, records, and critical tasks than on ensuring that employees, first, survive unharmed and, second, are physically and emotionally able to work.

This book describes how to plan, prepare for, and deal with the human side of workplace crises. In a crisis, employees express fear, shock, sadness, anger, and sometimes paralysis, often in erratic patterns. Once the initial shock has worn off and employees know that they and their families and friends are safe, they generally express a resiliency and resolve to return to work, but sometimes in an unpredictable manner. We must deal with these issues head on if we're to reassure our employees and restore stability to our organizations.

When employees' lives are at stake, our first priority is to protect them. Once we've ensured their safety, we have to make sure they *feel* safe. We also have to recognize that the reality of safety doesn't always match the perception for some people. In these traumatic situations, we face many challenges in helping employees establish a comfort zone and return to work. We're often dealing with the unknown. We also need to face and overcome our own fears. We should remember that, while it's demanding and challenging work, it can also be extremely rewarding.

I hope that reading this book will inspire you to take action. Starting now, you need to think about what you and your organization should do to incorporate the human component in your disaster preparedness plans. While protecting an organization's physical and intellectual property and maintaining business continuity are critical, HR's duty to safeguard people outweighs all other considerations when disaster strikes.

Susan R. Meisinger, SPHR
President and Chief Executive Officer
Society for Human Resource Management

Preface

Do you want to decrease your stress levels, limit trauma, and avoid agony when faced with a disaster at work? We're not talking about the garden-variety disaster you may encounter weekly, such as your computer crashing, your unreasonable deadline being moved up, or your having to fire an employee who doesn't fit with your culture. No, we're talking about dealing with such disasters as floods, murders, riots, bombings, earthquakes, hurricanes, pandemics, and CEO deaths and malfeasance.

Think this doesn't apply to you? Think again. We are anything but disaster fans, junkies, or authorities, but over our working careers we've personally experienced more workplace disasters than we ever imagined possible. In writing this book, we also talked with other HR leaders, communication professionals, operations executives, and other key personnel and listened to their stories. They faced some of the same as well as different disasters at their workplaces.

Why This Book?

We believe the chances are good that many of you will join our ranks before you retire. It's a dangerous world out there. This is not fatalistic thinking; we're just being practical. We'd like you to be disaster survivors too, and we want you to handle the unexpected with relative ease by following the lessons we and others have learned the hard way.

In response to our challenges, we took a range of actions. Many were successful, and some not so, as you'll read. We had to improvise along the way because, for the most part, we had no roadmap to follow. No book like this existed. Instead, we were guided by our courage to act and our commitment to make our employees safe and secure, to put our businesses back on track, and to restore some sense of normalcy to the workplace, all as soon as possible.

It's all too easy to put the planning on hold, claiming we don't have the time or resources for it, especially when there are so many more pressing issues on our plates at work. And if a plan *does* exist, it tends to focus on business operations, systems, and structural issues and tasks, ignoring the people side. In the years since September 11, 2001, many companies have recognized the need for planning. Also, a large number of guides have become available on how to establish and carry out emergency preparedness/business continuity plans, but they don't deal with the human issues.

In our experiences, the human side requires special care, consideration, and action. Certain emotional and psychological themes run through all of these disasters, whether a hurricane, flood, fire, earthquake, civil disturbance, shooting, terrorist attack, or act of corporate malfeasance. In the aftermath of such disasters, employees and their families are fearful, shocked, dismayed, paralyzed, saddened, angered—sometimes all at the same time, but more often in stages that are difficult to predict. After a time—which can range from hours to years—the affected individuals adopt an attitude of resolve and a desire to return to normalcy—although for them normalcy will never be the same.

Our goals with this book are to:

- Give you a jump-start to make sure you become involved in disaster planning and, when you do, you consider the people issues.
- Inspire you to take charge and lead during a disaster. This means taking an active rather than a passive role in planning the response to a disaster, dealing with the human issues of the disaster, and working to restabilize yourself, your employees, and your organization.
- Sensitize you regarding the people issues, and prepare you to anticipate employees' special emotional and psychological needs so you can deal with them quickly and begin to heal employees' hearts and minds.

The stories in this book cover a 20-year-span, but the same themes emerge. You could say we're getting older but not always better at dealing with the human issues in the wake of a crisis. Consequently, this book also serves as a wake-up call for all of us: the veterans of one or multiple crises, the planners who have escaped danger to date, and those who have been putting off the inevitable. We need to get actively involved in dealing with the people dimension of disasters.

The Audience for This Book

The "you" we address throughout this book include Human Resource leaders and staff members; communications professionals, including those responsible for employee communications and media relations; managers in general, and in particular those who want to assume a leadership role and build strong relationships with employees and other work colleagues; and employees who want to empower themselves.

You—especially the HR and communications professionals as well as the managers—all play a critical role in dealing with people issues in your day-to-day jobs. Your special skills are even more crucial in disaster preparedness and response efforts.

In times of crises, Human Resources and Public Relations—the two professions that most affect people inside and outside their organizations—need to adopt a special mindset. We need to view ourselves respectively as Human Relations and People Relations. When a disaster strikes, our primary role is to serve as leaders and protect people.

Despite all the differences between the sorts of disasters we and others have experienced, we have observed many common themes, starting with the number one, absolute requirement: **HR professionals must assume leadership in preparing for disasters and taking action when disasters strike, focusing especially on people issues.**

According to Libby Sartain, Senior Vice President of Human Resources and Chief People Yahoo at Yahoo! Inc., in the event of an emergency, HR leaders must be prepared to lead the leaders.[1]

We agree. We also think that others, especially communications professionals, need to be prepared as well. In the face of fear, it's human nature to want to flee. For the sake of employees and the organization, those who want to stay and fight—or those who reluctantly agree to stay and work—must rise to the challenge and deal with the crisis at hand.

One of the key questions that you have to answer for yourself—and this book can help you do that—is whether you have the capabilities for dealing with the dynamic situation a disaster presents, especially the need to remain on the scene and act as a leader.

There's one more point to note before jumping into the book. Many of the individuals who have shared their stories with us come from large companies. As a result, they have resources at their disposal that those of you at smaller organizations might not. That's no excuse for putting off planning or running from a disaster. Instead, you just need to be more creative about how you use outside help, which is often available at no or little cost. Throughout this book, we mention some resources and ideas to consider if you work for a small to mid-size company.

How to Use This Book

This book is an action guide, not a textbook, so use it in any way that will encourage you and help you act. You'll find that subjects such as communications, trauma counseling, and Employee Assistance Programs (EAPs) appear in several chapters rather than being covered comprehensively in individual chapters. We did this because communications, trauma, and the EAP are so intertwined in disaster planning/preparedness and business continuity planning that we wanted to reinforce integrated planning and execution.

The book is divided into three main sections.

Part I: Planning for Disasters

Specifically, this section covers:

- How to adopt the mindset needed to prepare for and deal with disasters, including making sure you have the necessary capabilities to act in the face of fear
- How to include the people perspective in your disaster planning
- What to consider in the creation of contingent HR policies

This section, especially Chapter 2, defines the basic terms used in the book, such as *business continuity plan* and *disaster*.

Part II: Dealing with Disasters

This section addresses:

- How to take care of employees, with the emphasis on their safety
- How to support managers and HR staff
- How to balance employee needs and get back to business
- How to get employees back on track
- How to start the healing process and then gain momentum with it
- Quick steps you can take immediately to help you plan effectively

The Resources Section

This section includes:

- Resources, including articles, books, and websites, to help you along the way
- A business continuity outline that can serve to jump-start your planning efforts
- A sample telephone tree for notifying people
- A sample wallet card detailing the actions to take in the event of a disaster
- Employee emergency response procedures
- Suggestions of what to do at home

Read—or, more realistically—skim the chapters and sections that interest you, in any order you want, with one exception: Start with the Prologue if you question the value of planning for and paying attention to disasters. The deluge of disasters that befell one of the authors in a short period of time should make you a believer in the benefits of disaster planning.

Use the index if you want to find particular topics.

Also check out the book's website at www.leadingpeoplethrough disasters.com, which includes a feedback section. We're interested in your ideas and suggestions and any steps you've taken, especially if they may be of benefit to others. A disaster is daunting enough without having to go it alone.

Principles to Live and Work By

For you to optimize the value of this book and successfully deal with disasters, especially their human aspect, we suggest you adopt these three principles:

1. *Have an emergency preparedness/business continuity plan.* You and your organization must have a comprehensive, multifaceted emergency preparedness/business continuity plan that focuses on the business issues, in addition to dealing with the human issues. No one can predict the type or timing of a disaster, but chances are great that *something* will happen sometime, and sooner than you might think. If you've got a plan, you'll be better able to respond to the situation and recover faster.

2. *Prepare to lead.* You must be prepared to assume a leadership role in planning for and taking action when disasters strike. This means taking the time to develop plans and executing them immediately when needed, without asking permission— especially where people's safety, security, and health are at stake. You need to recognize and remember you are in the best position to deal with the complex, unfolding human side of these events, both short- and long-term. Yet you must also realize you cannot do this alone. You must work closely with individuals from many disciplines, both inside and outside the organization.

3. *Expect the unexpected.* Regardless of how much planning you do, you must appreciate you will still experience the unexpected when a disaster strikes and you will have to adjust your plans on the fly. This may include propping up any of the organization's leaders who can't deliver in a crisis and supporting those who rise to the occasion. And these days it also may mean cleaning up after an executive or team of executives who caused or contributed to a man-made disaster, whether it involves corporate fraud, ethical lapses, insider trading, or some other type of malfeasance.

By adopting these principles and attending to the lessons we and others have learned the hard way, we hope you plan thoroughly, act quickly, and always show courage. Disasters require leaders.

Top Five Actions to Take:
Suggestions from a Veteran Incident Commander

If you aren't able to do anything else, veteran Incident Commander Jack Armstrong suggests focusing on these five actions:

- Having an effective emergency response plan
- Having secure backup, and an alternative download location for all essential electronic data
- Having a system for immediately contacting all customers and a plan for managing their needs
- Ensuring that you have home contact information for all employees
- Knowing the options for relocating your business

Authors' note: We hope you take the time to focus more on the human side.

Prologue

How HR Started Leading—First by Accident and Then by Design

Kathryn McKee

The following is a first-person account of how the Human Resources staff members of First Interstate Bancorp, First Interstate Bank of California, and First Interstate Bank Limited (since acquired by Wells Fargo) learned through their experiences with earthquakes, a building fire, and a civil disturbance to deal with crises and to lead their colleagues and employees through them.

Introduction

Human Resources leaders are constantly on call to solve unexpected problems: the need for a sudden staff reduction, rumors in the marketplace about a hostile takeover bid, and new, secret plans for management and organization changes. We drop whatever we're working on and dive into the new issue at hand, responding to the needs of our colleagues. Once the problem is solved, we go back to the pressing day-to-day work that we love.

Then, in the middle of the night, the phone rings. The voice on the other end says that the headquarters building is on fire, and asks what HR should do. Or there is a risk that the river that runs through your city may flood. What are the chances of this happening, and what are the possible consequences? Will your emergency preparedness plans be sufficient? Plans? What plans?

Or your CEO dies unexpectedly, and there is no succession plan. Or an ex-employee walks into the reception area with a gun, shoots and kills the staff there, and then walks into the Accounting Department and takes out a few others. What do you do in any of these scenarios?

You may have contingency plans for emergencies, but chances are the plans aren't as comprehensive as you need them to be. In October 2005 the Society for Human Resource Management published a survey on disaster preparedness.[1] Of the 314 organizations reporting, more than 75% said they had some form of disaster preparedness plan in place.

As for HR involvement, 18% of HR practitioners reporting said they were primarily responsible for the creation of the plans, and 31% participated equally in their creation; 29% stated they advised others; and 22% stated that they had no role. Where does your organization fall along this spectrum?

When it comes to a disaster of any kind and any magnitude, as a Human Resources practitioner—whether you are the Executive Vice President or the HR manager of a small company—you can't just *respond* to the call for action; you must help *lead* your leaders into action. This may be an unusual role that lies outside your comfort zone. However, it is our job to react to requests; in this case, we must be the leaders and initiators of action.

What follows is a true story of how our group of HR executives and subordinates responded to lead our organizations through a series of disasters and became very competent at it—first by accident and then by design.

It is a lesson that equipped us to deal with an earthquake, a building fire, two more earthquakes, a city-wide riot, and the 1993 bombing of the World Trade Center. Although you may never face an earthquake, you may be confronted with a fire, tornado, hurricane, riot, bombing, or some other disaster where you live or work.

Six Disasters in Seven Years
A Wake-up Call

In 1987 the Los Angeles area experienced a magnitude 5.9 earthquake. The top four Human Resources executives of then First

Interstate Bancorp were on the 6th floor of the 62-story First Interstate headquarters building. We were planning a huge reduction in the workforce, which in itself was a major transformation for our bank, when the building began to shake. Employees in the adjacent cafeteria started screaming and running for the stairs. It was very scary.

As a result, the City of Los Angeles mandated disaster planning, and First Interstate Bancorp set about developing its first emergency preparedness/business continuity plan. HR participated in a very passive way. We were team members assigned the task of planning what occupants of each floor in the building would do, establishing floor wardens and toe taggers, and arranging for emergency food and water; we knew that in the event of another quake, we could be in the building for up to seven days.

What HR *didn't* do was think through how employees might react; we did not link the trauma of what we had just been through with the essential elements that should form the foundation of the plan. We did not lead the effort—we just reacted.

About six months later, we participated in an earthquake drill to test the new business continuity plan; food and medical supplies were in place, and walkie-talkies and radios were operational. Wardens put on hard hats and vests, and all employees practiced where to go and what to do. The Emergency Operations Center (EOC) was activated. Everything worked: we were ready for the "Big One"!

Three weeks after this test, on a Wednesday evening, the "Big One" turned out to be a fire in the headquarters building. Many of the employees learned about the fire while watching the 11 o'clock news. Some were driving home from a downtown black-tie event and saw it firsthand. They pounced on their car telephones and started calling fellow employees.

It was incomprehensible to see flames shooting out of the 12th floor, where our bond and currency trading businesses were located. The business continuity plan went into effect immediately. While the fire was still raging, managers were setting up the Emergency Operations Center, and they had it ready by midnight; they began manning the phones and following the plan to the letter. We quickly found space at a nearby hotel and established a press center.

Twenty-four hours later, the bank's Trust Division had been relocated, and the traders from the 12th floor were on planes to the bank's New York, London, and Tokyo offices. Trading is a 24-hour-a-day operation, and it can't stop, so this aspect of the business was in relatively good shape.

But Thursday morning there was confusion among the employees who worked in the headquarters building, who did not know what to do or where to go. *If* these instructions had been included in the business continuity plan, they had not been well communicated. We had not planned for a total building evacuation; we did not have a master list of telephone numbers for the 13,000 employees in several California subsidiaries, or even the 3,000 affected by the fire. We were able, however to re-create a telephone directory almost overnight, and within two days we had an employee master list.

It may seem incredible in the 21st century that these lists did not exist, but in 1988 First Interstate had no enterprise software system. And your own human resources/payroll systems may not have this capability even now.

By Friday, office equipment had been ordered. By Saturday, emergency space planning had been completed and all employees notified where to report on Monday morning. An all-hands meeting took place on Saturday. There were more questions than answers, but we all muddled through; employees were clearly relieved to learn of the enormous planning effort taking place.

On Monday morning all affected employees reported to new offices, cubicles, and conference rooms. In many cases, one cubicle had been assigned to as many as six people. Some employees were sitting on the floor with nothing to do because their work papers, files, calendars, daybooks, computers, and printers were in the building, and we could not get to them.

A new culture developed immediately. Banks tend to be rule bound, protocol is paramount, and status is determined by the size and location of one's office. With the fire, the rule book was thrown out. The CEO of the bank was put in a tiny office. A special language was created: we had an "EOC," "guests," and "hosts." The hosts provided coffee and donuts. Pizzas appeared, a strong camaraderie emerged, and there was incredible cooperation. It was a bit like summer camp: new friends, new places, improvisation, and excitement.

HR Steps Up

Two days later we were still cramped and crowded. People were beginning to feel anger and frustration from not being able to do their jobs properly. Summer camp was over! Everyone realized that we would not get back into the building for a long, long time, and the situation had become more than our employees could bear. They were not only angry and frustrated; they were also frightened, irritable, distressed, and sad, and they could not concentrate.

The standard response by Human Resources had been to seek permission to take action, so we went to the CEOs of the three affected business units. They gave us free rein; they said we should do whatever was right for our employees and not worry about putting together the usual detailed business case to justify our actions.[2] So that is what we did. The CEOs' commitment to the employees allowed us to balance the potential conflict between protecting the corporate interests in medical, insurance, and legal matters and caring for our people.

Within days of the fire, we had assembled a group of HR staff to determine what support was needed from HR, public affairs, communications, and security. Soon we had a plan and were moving quickly from ideas to action.

We did not wait to be asked for help; we became innovative and freed ourselves from the bureaucratic culture within which we normally functioned. The HR staffs from the three entities joined together, highly motivated to create and deliver programs as quickly as possible. The previous method of working together had been to use committees—endlessly—and avoid decision making, if possible by bucking a decision up to a higher authority. The staffs now felt empowered to act, and they did.

Dealing with Trauma

Employees expressed anger, apprehension, frustration, and grief over what had occurred. They felt that their trust had been violated because all of the procedures they had learned to follow in case of a fire seemed to have failed. For example, we had been trained to use the fire stairways because they would be smoke free. But the air system, which was designed to blow smoke out of the stairways, had not worked during the fire. Even though only four employees were in the building that night, the continuing refrain was "If we'd been at work, we'd have died." Logic suggests that if they had been at work, they would have used the fire extinguishers and quickly put the fire out, but logic does not prevail in the midst of trauma.

A sense of futility was also expressed. A typical remark was "How can I produce my usual quality of work when I have no tools, no files, no computer database, no calendar, and no phone directory? I can't keep this up!" At this time, laptop computers were not readily available and people were not accustomed to telecommuting; we did not have e-mail, cell phones (other than car phones), or other now common electronic devices. (However, even if your organization has the latest technology, there's no guarantee that employees will have the devices with them when disaster strikes or that the technology will work as planned.)

Because we worked for a bank, we knew the value of trauma counseling and had offered it in the branches where robberies had occurred. We knew that psychological trauma was now present to varying degrees, depending on how the individual work unit was affected. Clearly, those few employees who were in the building during the fire needed special counseling to deal with their deep personal concerns. However, other groups needed counseling with different emphases:

- The trauma was magnified if a person was already suffering from some other high-impact event such as a divorce or death; we had to make special efforts immediately to deal with such complications.
- Employees working outside the downtown area had to learn to make allowances for those who had been dislocated. This tendency was operative in all of the other disasters we had encountered. Watch for it if your business has multiple locations. Those not directly affected do not understand what their fellow employees are going through and may chide or tease, or, at the other extreme, be overly solicitous.
- Employees in downtown locations who were now sharing their spaces with guest employees could become resentful of those who had invaded their space.
- Employees who were displaced by the fire were feeling violated by the failure of the fire suppression systems in the building.

- Staff support groups responsible for responding to the crisis and taking action had to rise above their own emotional reactions. (This is discussed in Chapter 1.)
- The senior leadership team responsible for directing the action had to make moment-by-moment decisions with no frame of reference. We all had to learn to operate in new and different ways. This helped us to become more effective change agents and leaders.

Within days we had hired a number of trauma counselors to begin a comprehensive program of debriefing all affected work units. Group sessions were mandatory and were supplemented by individual counseling through our Employee Assistance Program and outside referrals as deemed necessary. Face-to-face meetings were held in which employees learned to deal with their feelings.

The Counseling Programs

An Employee Assistance Program (EAP), which is a type of behavioral health management program, is used to help employees manage difficult personal or professional issues that may be hindering their ability to perform. The trauma brought on by a disaster can cause or exacerbate individual problems.

Throughout this book, we refer to EAPs and trauma counseling. Chapter 8 explains the use of EAPs.

This step was seen as an absolutely critical piece of the recovery program. Not only was it an effort to reach out and assuage the anger, sadness, fear, and frustration felt by employees, but it also allowed the EAP staff to identify potential workers' compensation problems and take action to seek immediate help for those people who needed it. The confidential debriefing sessions also helped us develop a blueprint for action.

Communications and Training

The HR staff recognized a need to develop communication vehicles that would be honest, direct, and timely, explaining what was known and when it was known. A special publication, *Briefing*, was published twice a week and contained news of fire inspections and cleaning, instructions to staff, and honest answers to the questions employees were asking.

Because supervisors needed help in coping with lowered productivity as well as high stress levels and their manifestations—for example, fatigue, absenteeism, and anger—a special manual was prepared for them, and the HR staff implemented small-group meetings to teach them about the process. (Excerpts from this manual are provided in Chapter 6.)

An ad hoc "policy committee" was established in the month after the fire to develop policy statements; these were subsequently printed and distributed to all affected employees. (Policy updates are covered in Chapter 3.)

Helping employees to feel acknowledged and appreciated was deemed important. Managers applied less pressure toward achieving business standards, and employees were encouraged to have picnics and "casual" days. Many managers gave each of their employees a "mental health" day, saying, "Just take a day off; it won't count against your vacation."

An "employee morale committee" was established to plan employee events, and this gave management the opportunity to thank employees for putting up with so many inconveniences—cramped quarters, lack of personal space, no tools. A picnic was planned for June; there the CEOs of the affected organizations, aided by other senior executives and staff members, cooked hamburgers in an effort to provide some fun and relaxation and encourage a change in the employees' mindset. The theme was "Meeting the Challenge, Thanks to You," and the activity was greatly appreciated by all who attended.

Lines of communication also had to be opened up to customers. The bank's main branch in Los Angeles was closed for the four months it took to restore the building to its original beauty and also improve its functionality. Branch employees contacted their customers and made arrangements for their business to be transacted at other First Interstate branches in the downtown area.

A carefully prepared advertising campaign, emphasizing safety and customer service, was used to educate the public about the building's recovery and the branch's return to business. We took great care to keep our emphasis between customer service and employee welfare in balance.

Reentry

For some time after the fire there was uncertainty regarding the structural integrity of the building, although the building's steel passed the most stringent stress-tolerance tests. The building's safety remained the key issue for employees as plans were made in August to return to the site in September, four months after the fire.

The staff planned a program around many of the safety concerns that had surfaced early on. Just after Labor Day, detailed reentry plans were in place, and the CEO and other senior holding-company executives became the first group to move back into the building. It was an impressive event: the branch held a grand re-opening, where "Welcome Home" banners greeted returning tenants, employees, and clients.

But there was more to the reentry than just a festive homecoming. The fear experienced by some employees resurfaced. The same questions of safety and security were raised all over again. Along with the festivities, a special orientation program was provided to educate employees about the building and why it was safe to reenter. Meetings were held for every group of employees just before they were scheduled to move back into the building.

At these orientation meetings a panel of experts, including the building's architect and structural engineer, a safety expert, a representative of building security, and a moderator from HR, informed the groups in great detail about the structural integrity of the building. The HR staff went on hard-hat tours beforehand to become knowledgeable about the structure and the testing, and HR or EAP staff were stationed on each floor as people reported back to the tower.

Booklets about the building and its safety provisions were sent to each employee's home. A videotape about the building was produced, an open house was held so that families could come and see for themselves, and a special issue of *Briefing* was published.

Trauma counselors were available for anxious employees. A policy was put in place for those who could not bring themselves to return to the building. The HR staff were highly visible during those first few weeks back to help people deal with whatever issues were troubling them. Ultimately, we returned to our regular rhythm of work.

The Earth Moved—Again

About a year after we had moved back into the building, San Francisco suffered a massive, magnitude 7.1 earthquake. Buildings burned, people were killed, and houses and freeways crumbled.

Because of the lessons learned from the Whittier Narrows quake, First Interstate's Emergency Operations Center was up and running in a matter of minutes. The bank's branches in the Bay Area were inspected as soon as possible. Using a telephone tree, managers called employees that night and told them what to do the following day. (A sample telephone tree is included in the Resources section on page 144.) People were to report for work or stay home as instructed. We thought all the bases had been covered.

Within a day, however, we found out that several employees were missing. No answer at home, no information from the emergency contacts in the files. We called the morgues and hospitals until these employees remembered to alert us that they were alive and safe.

We realized immediately we needed to give the most basic of instructions and provide a more complete listing of emergency contacts; we also gained a stronger awareness that it is critical to have *everyone* check in. First Interstate then issued booklets to all employees giving explicit instructions—by branch or office location—on what to do, whom to call, and where to go in case of any type of emergency.

We set up counseling sessions for employees who needed help, and assisted employees who found themselves permanently or temporarily homeless. We also worked with affected supervisors and managers to help them understand why some employees were having difficulty concentrating: they simply had not been prepared for the emotional shock.

It is crucial for managers to understand that individuals recover from traumatic events on their own timelines and in their own ways. As a result of the previous earthquake and the building fire, we had learned to make generous use of purchased guidebooks for employees and managers on dealing with stress, and we offered group and individual trauma counseling.

Slowly, our lives returned to normal. But when the wind blew strongly and the building swayed, people on the top floors became nervous, and our now well-trained supervisors and managers would move immediately to calm them.

Consequently, in 1994, when the devastating, magnitude 6.7 Northridge quake occurred in the Los Angeles Basin, we knew what to do. Even though there was severe damage, with freeways collapsing and businesses interrupted, our managers swung quickly into action, reassuring employees and offering counseling. We were back to business in a very short time.

A Riot Breaks Out

Rodney King was clocked at 100 miles per hour as he was chased by the Los Angeles police in March 1991. After he was stopped, a private citizen videotaped the police brutally beating him for about six minutes. As a result of 56 baton blows and six kicks, he sustained 11 skull fractures plus brain and kidney damage. The trial of the police officers began in March 1992, and in April an all-white jury convened in a white suburb found the officers not guilty.

The verdict immediately led to a riot. It began in South Central Los Angeles, a predominantly African-American neighborhood, spread quickly throughout the city into other ethnic neighborhoods, and then extended to other cities in the LA basin.

Employees at First Interstate Bank were working at their offices throughout the basin when the riots broke out, and many became anxious to get home as quickly as possible. Some lived in the areas affected, and many of those who lived elsewhere would have to drive through the mobs, fires, and crowded streets to reach their homes.

It was a harrowing experience. After making certain that everyone else had left the building, the HR staff went home By now we were experts at crisis response, so we ramped up the Employee Assistance Program, began a program of trauma counseling, and set about helping affected employees to cope. Despite all the support we were able to muster for them, employees remained afraid. Their work was hampered, use of sick leave soared, and it was generally difficult for all concerned. Finally, the riots were contained, the fires were put out, and life returned to what we had come to know as normal.

Although we had not created a specific plan for a civil disturbance, we had our business continuity plan and consequently had the EOC up and running. It seemed that no matter how good we became at disaster planning, there was always some event that had not been considered, and riots were the latest.

When a second trial of the police officers was announced, we prepared for Act II and Corporate Security quickly developed a civil disturbance plan. The officers were found guilty, and there were no further riots.

We went on with our lives until October 3, 1995, when the O.J. Simpson verdict was due. We were ready. The civil disturbance plan was in effect, and we all knew what to do in case he was found guilty. Again, we were glued to the TV—this time in our workplace— fascinated not just as human beings but as HR leaders, ready to spring into action if need be.

A Man-made Disaster

In 1993 a bomb went off in one of the World Trade Center's underground garages. At this time I was Senior Vice President and Region Head of HR for Standard Chartered Bank (SCB), based in Los Angeles. SCB had a gold trading function located in the World Trade Center. The HR Director there worked with the Managing Director to ensure that all employees were evacuated safely. Their actions were successful, and the employees were able to return to work in a few days. We called the HR Director immediately to arrange for trauma counseling for all, and we were told, "We don't need that California stuff: We're New Yorkers!" She was serious; we trusted her judgment, and no counseling was utilized.

Because of this experience, on September 11, 2001, when the SCB employees located in 7 World Trade Center—across the street from the Twin Towers—felt the ground shake, they knew in their hearts what had happened. They walked down 47 flights of stairs to the ground floor, and then, following their business continuity plan, either went home or walked to the Hudson River Ferry. There they had the ash washed off their clothing. A core group of employees, still dripping wet, went to work in the EOC in New Jersey, a true tribute to strength of character and good planning.

Lessons Learned

By the end of this seven-year period, I as an HR leader and my colleagues had dramatically changed our behavior. We had become leaders in the face of disaster. We were the drivers behind the development and implementation of disaster-related employee policies, working as full partners with the emergency planners. We did not wait to be asked, nor did we ask for permission or forgiveness. Senior leaders and middle managers expected us to swing into action in response to any crisis that occurred. We would stabilize the situation and ensure the safety, security, and well-being of our employees. Employees knew we were there for them. In hindsight, it was an epiphany for all: we had developed and applied critical new skills that were invaluable to the bank and its employees.

The lessons we learned can be condensed into the following list:

1. Step up to a leadership role in anticipating the human issues you might face in the event of a catastrophe; you can't wait to be asked. You must insert yourself into the business continuity planning process even if you have not been invited or allowed to participate in the past. You can be an invaluable partner to the senior leadership team and line managers.

   Think through now how you can step in if executives and managers crumble in the face of disaster. What skills and resources do you have or do you need to develop in order to be the calming agent? (See Chapter 1 for a discussion of this topic.) It's your job to reassure and to keep people on track. Your self-control will have a calming influence, and employees at all levels will look to you for reassurance and a plan of action.

2. Be a champion for business continuity planning, and be involved in reviewing it regularly. (See Chapter 2 for details.)

   a. Make sure the plan addresses the human components of a crisis, including what provisions must be made for the care of employees near and far.

   b. Make sure the plan incorporates a variety of scenarios and that you practice them using either tabletop, virtual, or live–action enactments.

   c. Prepare a telephone tree or similar scheme for contacting employees. All managers should keep a list at home of their employees' home telephone and cell phone numbers, and their home and second-home addresses.

   d. Have a plan in place for creating an ad hoc telephone directory once employees have been relocated.

   e. Develop a space plan for any type of disaster. To the extent possible, know in advance where and when employees will report to work and where alternative work sites will be. Scout out rentable space, and maintain a list of furniture and office equipment suppliers.

3. Develop contingent HR policies. It will save an enormous amount of time if you and the senior team can agree before a catastrophe on how you wish to care for your employees: what you are willing to pay for and not pay for, what you can give them, what to reimburse them for, and the like. (See Chapter 3 for sample policies.)

4. Over-communicate. Answer questions about safety frankly, promptly, and often. Be aware of what communication vehicles you have or can develop quickly, as well as what staff are available for getting a variety of messages to employees quickly.

5. Know what employee assistance resources are available and how they can be implemented to head off potential trauma-related problems. For example, as described in Chapter 8:

   a. Be acutely sensitive to human trauma, and go overboard with help rather than ignoring potential personal problems.

   b. Understand how the event may have affected employees' families. Plan for extra assistance or trauma counseling for severe cases.

6. Make symbolic efforts to build and preserve credibility. For example, in the case of a work site that has undergone a significant amount of damage, move your most senior managers back to the site first. That not only makes a statement about safety, but indicates that they believe they are not at risk. Employees may or may not yet believe that all is okay, and this is a first step to soothe their anxieties.

7. Healing is slow process; not everyone will be on the same page at a given stage. Patience is helpful, and a strong yet understanding approach by managers will go a long way toward getting their people back on track.

Part I

Planning
for Disasters

This section discusses the following topics:

- The roles and responsibilities of Human Resources managers, line managers, communications staff members, and others in the planning effort and when faced with a disaster; the leadership capabilities one needs in order to lead a business continuity planning effort, and those needed when one is facing a disaster.
- How to prepare for and lead the business continuity planning effort; where to go for basic information; what should be included, and what pieces of the plan small companies should concentrate on in their planning efforts; and how to protect the plan against failure.
- What policies the planning team should consider when developing the business continuity plan. By having policies in place before a disaster, those responding to a disaster will save an enormous amount of time and will be free to make critical decisions on the fly.

Chapter 1

Preparing to Lead in the Face of Fear

This chapter covers four topics:

When planning for a disaster:
- Identifying the players as well as their roles and responsibilities for planning
- Recognizing the competencies (such as skills, knowledge, and attributes) that can help you be an effective leader

When dealing with a disaster:
- Reviewing the roles and responsibilities of the various players
- Understanding what leadership competencies are necessary in the face of fear, especially in a disaster situation

Overview

On a scale of 1 to 10, how prepared are you to deal with a disaster befalling your organization? Are you ready to lead your employees through it? Are you geared up to deal with a hurricane, fire, flood, tornado, murder, chemical spill, act of corporate malfeasance, flu pandemic, terrorist attack, or some other type of disaster?

On second thought, maybe you'd prefer to close this book and take a pleasure trip. How about a cruise down the Mississippi River, where you'll end up in New Orleans? You'll find yourself in the state of Louisiana, which in August 2005 was actually "the state of denial," according to Charles Pizzo and Gerard Braud, two crisis communications experts and Hurricane Katrina victims.

"And if you're not thinking about or planning what you might do in a crisis situation now, you're in a state of denial too. There are just too many risks out there," Pizzo warns.

One good sign that you're not in the state of denial is that you have this book open. We hope you're ready for the challenge. Our goal is to excite you to action so you will take a leadership role within your organization and prepare for the worst, with the hope that nothing bad actually happens. However, the odds are that you will face some kind of minor or major crisis in the course of your work life.

Preparing for a Disaster
Identifying the Players and Their Roles and Responsibilities

In business continuity planning, one of the critical leadership tasks is defining the roles and responsibilities of the key members of management who will be involved in planning for and managing a disaster. This section details the processes to be carried out by individuals in the roles of CEO, CFO, Human Resources Director, Communications Officer, and other selected members of the management team. The job titles and organizational structure of your company may differ from the generic positions described here, but this summary will give you an idea of the division of responsibilities.

Most senior executive: Chief Executive Officer/ General Manager/other title

- Mandates the development and implementation of a business continuity plan
- Appoints the core team, announcing and expressing confidence in its members and emphasizing their delegation to a high level of independent thinking
- Meets with the core team from time to time for updates and to offer advice and counsel

Incident Commander

- Reports to the CEO
- Develops the Incident Command System, which specifies who will do what tasks in the case of an incident (emergency, crisis, disaster, catastrophe, etc.)

- Takes charge in case of a disaster and is the sole contact with emergency responders, such as firefighters, police, and hazmat (hazardous materials) team
- Addresses the media on-site covering the disaster, as he or she is on the line and has the most up-to-date information on the situation, unless another individual is designated to be the spokesperson

Chief Financial Officer/Controller/other title for financial executive

- Works with the core team to develop the *business case* for planning, including the return on investment. Consider the costs of planning, such as:
  a. Possible use of an outside expert on emergency preparedness or business continuity planning
  b. Downtime (i.e., time away from job duties, spent in meetings, information gathering, etc.; or due to dislocation of work or loss of property) and its impact on the profitability or viability of the business
  c. Materials, equipment, and supplies, including food and water, cots, blankets, radiophones, walkie-talkies, satellite phones, extra cell phones, 800 number for an employee "cool line," and special website
  d. Possible off-site space for an emergency operations center (see Chapter 2)
  e. Backup information technology and telecommunications systems
  f. Trauma counseling or Employee Assistance Program (EAP) (see Prologue and Chapter 8) and returning employees to reasonable levels of productivity

Core team
The core team will develop the strategies and policies that will be used to develop contingency plans for a short business interruption (e.g., a few hours); a disaster, where business is interrupted for a few days; and a major catastrophe, where

business is interrupted for the foreseeable future, with no identifiable end date. Core team members and their responsibilities are:

Human Resources

- Working with the core team to identify the Incident Commander and others who will take charge in case of a disaster
- Defining roles and responsibilities for the various individuals who will staff the Emergency Operations Center (see Chapter 2)
- Developing contingency plans for the relocation of employees under a variety of scenarios
- Instructing the core team about Human Resources philosophy and how the organization can care for its workforce through contingent HR policies, as well as developing contingency HR policies (explained in Chapter 3)
- Developing the executive emergency contact list, which specifies who gets alerted and when
- Arranging for the contingent use of external behavioral health consultants or an Employee Assistance Program (EAP) (see Chapter 8)
- Developing a telephone tree or other electronic notification system along with collateral materials so that employees at all levels of the organization know whom to call, where to go, when to stay home, and what other actions to take
- Ascertaining the need to deploy staff in other parts of the United States or the world to keep the business running

Safety Officer or security (if applicable)

- Developing a variety of scenarios that could result in business interruption and coordinating these scenarios with communications facilities
- Developing evacuation procedures as well as specific procedures for such disasters as a fire, flood, hurricane, tornado, chemical spill, or explosion, and setting up a "shelter in place" (i.e., a place in the facility where employees can go for shelter rather than leaving the facility and risking exposure)

Operations/production (if applicable)

- Developing contingency plans for inventory, manufacturing, distribution, and other functions in case of evacuation
- Identifying a location to borrow or rent space
- Determining the feasibility of moving the warehouse, production, and distribution functions
- Analyzing the consequences of a short- or medium-term inability to deliver products/services to customers

Communications

- Creating a crisis communications plan that dovetails with the business continuity plan and includes key messages for each scenario in the business continuity plan
- Developing a media strategy for minor and major crises
- Working closely with the Incident Commander to determine who will serve as the company spokesperson, depending on the situation, and clarify who speaks, when, and to whom, internally and externally; also, providing advance media training for these individuals, if needed
- Maintaining ongoing good relations with the press, especially the radio and TV newscasters in the local markets, and preparing press releases and organizing press conferences as necessary
- Developing employee communication templates and determining the best distribution system for the communications under different disaster scenarios
- Working with the Safety Officer to develop response plans for a variety of disaster scenarios (e.g., short- or long-term power outage, explosion, chemical spill, or other foreseeable event, given the type of business) and coordinating closely with other core team members as well as with the entire planning team
- Coordinating closely with HR and Safety officers when a disaster strikes

Business continuity planning team

This team develops detailed business continuity plans and tactics for each major function in the organization. For an outline of the topics to be considered, refer to the Resources section on page 141. Depending on the management structure, functions also may include:

Information technology

- Developing system backup plans and arranging for backup sites for data storage
- Developing backup plans for all telecommunications devices, including instructions on how phone lines are to be redirected to other sites and the establishment of toll-free numbers
- Developing IT network backup plans and testing protocols

Engineering, marketing, sales, and customer relations

- Developing specific business continuity plans
- Agreeing to take direction from the Incident Commander initially, when disaster strikes, and until the Incident Commander returns control to the management hierarchy
- Confirming that functional managers have made appropriate plans and have the necessary supplies to take care of employees

Legal

- Ensuring that the plan complies with federal and state safety and security regulations
- Verifying that workplace laws and regulations have been addressed (provisions for disabled employees, confidentiality of records, etc.)

Competent Business Planning Leadership

Leadership qualities for business continuity planning, as for any other aspect of business, start with the basics: *your self-image* and *your attitude* about what you know and what you can do. Do you see yourself as a leader or a follower? Do you take the initiative or do you suffer from the "dancing school syndrome," waiting to be asked?

The self-assessment grid starting on page 28 offers a good starting point for you to take stock of your leadership skills.

What drives leaders?

There is nothing more exhilarating than to be in the presence of great leaders. They motivate you to go where you did not even know you wanted to go. They inspire a shared vision, model the way, enable others to act, and encourage the heart.[1] What is it within people that enables them not just to lead well in normal times but, when faced with a crisis, to quickly overcome their own fear and shock and rise to the occasion, leading their people through the difficulty that is facing them?

What competencies (i.e., skills, knowledge attributes, and abilities) constitute leadership? Are different sets of skills and behaviors required for preparing and leading, versus responding in the face of a disaster? What does it take to face your own fear and, in spite of it, lead others through the crisis to the successful conclusion and beyond?

Wayne Brockbank is a partner with David Ulrich and others in charge of the 30,000-case Human Resource Competency model, which is featured in Ulrich's *Human Resource Champions* (1997) and Brockbank and Ulrich's *Competencies for the New HR* (2003). Dr. Brockbank spent some time with us to answer the question "What capabilities does one need to lead the business continuity planning and preparation phase?" He suggested that the following competencies are needed in the planning process:

Competency	Abilities and attributes
Strategic decision making*	Ability to: ▪ Identify problems that are central to the business strategy ▪ Lead strategic planning efforts ▪ Set the direction of change ▪ Have a vision for the future of the business Attributes ▪ Self-confidence ▪ Risk taking

Culture management	Ability to: ■ Help the organization define the culture required to meet the demands of external customers ■ Define the culture that is necessary to make the business strategy work ■ Build the culture that excites employees to action ■ Align HR practices (e.g., staffing, development, rewards and compensation) to the culture, for both regular business and pre-planning for a disaster
Market-driven connectivity	Ability to: ■ Disseminate customer information on a large scale ■ Leverage customer information in integrating the functional organization ■ Build the customer-focused workforce environment ■ Reduce information that inhibits focus on the customer
Fast change	Ability to: ■ Manage quickly and make fast decisions ■ Facilitate change processes ■ Ensure resource availability for change efforts ■ Measure the effectiveness of change ■ Adapt learning about change to new change initiatives ■ Determine when and how to modify a change in direction, both in regular operations and in a disaster

---

*Strategic decision making is an area where many HR and communications professionals don't believe in their own power; instead they sit back and wait to be asked. (And then some complain that they are not getting asked to the table!) The Society for Human Resource Management, the American Society for Training and Development, the American Management Association, the University of Michigan, the RBL Group, and the Center for Creative Leadership all offer outstanding courses in leadership skill building.

Dealing with a Disaster
Roles and Responsibilities

Your worst fears have been realized: Your organization is facing a disaster—a flash flood, chemical spill, or, even worse, an explosion and building collapse—that occurred late at night, so only the security guards were on the premises and, luckily, none of them was injured. What must be done and who will do it?

CEO

- Works with the Incident Commander, who has ordered the opening of the Emergency Operations Center (EOC, discussed in Chapter 2) in a space off-site
- May be relocated to the EOC to be able to continue to resolve business issues
- Provides the media with information developed by the Communications Officer
- Is accessible to employees to provide reassurance and demonstrate decisive leadership

Incident Commander

- Takes charge of managing the incident (crisis, disaster, etc.)
- Contacts emergency responders and solely provides direction
- May assign a second-in-command to run the EOC while he or she is at the site of the disaster
- Runs the disaster team, including representatives from operations, safety, Human Resources, and communications
- Provides instantaneous, up-to-date, and accurate public information to the media from an on-site vantage point
- Returns managing responsibilities to the management hierarchy as soon as practicable

Chief Financial Officer

- May be assigned to the EOC as a team member

Head of operations/production

- May be assigned to the EOC as a team member

Human Resources

- May have a department member assigned to the EOC

- HR leader assesses the situation with Incident Commander and CEO, and makes recommendations regarding employee needs
- Depending on the severity of the situation, HR leader recommends implementation of contingent policies (discussed in Chapter 3)
- Assigns staff to 24-hour coverage of telephone "cool line" and other electronic communications to answer employee questions, assuage fears, and the like

---

A "cool line" is a specific 800 number that employees can access for honest answers to their questions; it also serves as a "rumor control" center. This frees up the emergency hotline to disseminate directions for what to do, when, and where.

- May recommend all-hands meeting(s) to reassure employees and give them up-to-the-minute information
- May recommend individual or group counseling or screening depending on the severity of the situation (more on this in Chapter 8)

Communications Officer

- Works with the Incident Commander and CEO to make sure the organization speaks with one voice and delivers a message that is consistent and clear
- Prepares and distributes appropriate communications pieces for external audiences, including media, customers, vendors/suppliers, and investors
- Partners with HR to refine and distribute employee communications appropriate for the severity and duration of the disaster

Planning team members

- Put the detailed plans spelled out in the official business continuity document into operation
- As required, may be assigned to the EOC or to other duties as spelled out in the plan

Employees
- Follow the instructions given, ideally on their emergency response wallet card
- Stay in touch via the "cool line," website, or other telecommunications vehicle, or go to predetermined location for printed materials in case of a community power outage

Facing a Disaster Head On

What if the disaster you prepared for—or, the more likely scenario, another type of disaster—rocks your world? Do different leadership competencies come into play during a crisis? Probably not, but you will face a situation colored with emotion, and how you deal with this is what separates effective and successful leaders from those who stumble.

Richard E. Boyatzis,[2] co-author of *Resonant Leadership* and *Primal Leadership: Realizing the Power of Emotional Intelligence*, and Professor of Organizational Behavior at the Weatherhead School of Management at Case Western Reserve University, identifies three competencies that are key in times of crisis:

- *Mindfulness*
  Emotional awareness
  Empathy
  A keen sense of one's surroundings
- *Self-awareness*
- *Self-control*

People will be looking to you for leadership, so Dr. Boyatzis says you need both self-awareness and self-control to:

- Think quickly.
- Remain somewhat dispassionate, at least on the surface.
- Instill hope through verbal and nonverbal means.

This is not the time for that "deer in the headlights" look.

Taking a Look at Yourself

We've created a simple self-assessment grid that combines the ideas of Wayne Brockbank and Richard Boyatzis, as well as definitions from other competency models. We encourage you to jot down the assessments of your strengths and then note what you might do to further improve your capabilities.

Are You Ready to Lead?

Behavioral attributes:
Those qualities that come from within and have an impact on your behavior

Competency	How satisfied am I with my strengths in this area?	What can I do about it?
Initiative: Readiness to act and seize opportunities		
Relationship management: Inspirational leadership, influence, catalyst for change, conflict management, networking, teamwork and collaboration		
Self-awareness: Awareness of your emotions and their impact, knowledge of your strengths and weaknesses, sense of self-confidence		
Self-control: Ability to control emotions, maintain objectivity, be empathetic, attain a degree of dispassion		
Innovation: Creativity, tangential or peripheral thinking		

Skills, knowledge, and abilities that you learn

Competency	How satisfied am I with my strengths in this area?	What can I do about it?
Strategic planning: Creating a vision; mission and key strategies to move the business forward		
Tactical planning and organizing: Developing action plans, structure, and staffing so that the strategies can come to life		
Communication and interpersonal skills: Getting your message across to others; building relationships; remaining open to others' input		
Project management: Leading others in the execution of a short-term project; understanding PERT and Gantt charting; task and staff scheduling; critical path analysis		

If there are areas in the self-assessment grid where you feel you need some professional development, check the Leadership readings in the Resources section starting on page 136.

Using the Power of Denial to Face the Crisis

Often, the human reaction to a crisis is "This cannot be happening. This is unreal!" People may be stunned by what they are seeing or experiencing. It's as if the mind stops trying to comprehend the shock or horror of the event. In some cases, people run away, an instinct known as "fight or flight," because we as humans are compelled to seek safety or refuge when faced with danger. In other cases, we decide to tough it out, to fight back, to gain control of the situation as best we can. For example, when he witnessed the horror of September 11, 2001, occurring right across the street from his office, William Nickey, the Northeast Region Human Resources Director at Deloitte & Touche USA, says,

> My first reaction to this event—in my heart—was that I had to get home to Long Island to be with my family. But then my mind took over, and I told myself I had a job to do. Looking back, I realize now that I was in shock for the first 48 hours, but I made it through, not only playing my role as HR Director but also becoming a Disaster Recovery Project leader. Deloitte and Touche began immediately to make contact with all of our people, and miraculously, we lost only one employee who had not made it out of the World Trade Center.

In a crisis, we are compelled to act out of fear, confronted by the immediate threat of the situation. Mory Framer, a pioneer in trauma counseling, says that this inner resource is actually denial and that through denial we can regain control over the situation. What irony! Those who are effective in leading in the face of a disaster are in denial too. But because they encounter the denial at this stage, rather than doing so earlier and consequently avoiding the planning phase, they are able to help their organizations as opposed to putting them at undue risk.

Dr. Framer says, "The human condition gives great impetus to action through the fight/flight syndrome. When we don't or won't flee, we fight (within ourselves) to regain control in order to help others. The trauma or disruption we are facing creates *internal energy* that can be used to regain self-control."

A second insight from Dr. Framer is that employees, family members, friends, and colleagues may not react to or recover from a fearful situation as quickly as successful leaders do. It's necessary to understand and allow for this dynamic in the human side of emergency planning. Managers must be careful not to assume that their employees are gaining control as quickly as they are. You'll learn more about this in Part II, especially in Chapters 4 to 8.

Remaining Detached versus Getting Connected

Consider adding another ability to your behavioral toolkit, one that Stephen Schoonover, an expert in developing organizational competency models, refers to as *containment*. Containment enables you to:

- Set boundaries for behaviors and actions by yourself and others.
- Calm people by means of a soothing voice and other methods.
- Establish control through the use of a firm voice.
- Find ways to break the tension through emotional release, for example, by talking about the incident or finding a reason to laugh (dark humor) so people can begin healing. Jack Armstrong, a veteran fire chief and Incident Commander, says that dark humor is what helps keep people in balance in very trying times.

As a strong leader you need to be somewhat dispassionate. Yet you also have to be connected to those around you—empathetic and psychologically present without seeming detached. For example, practice the ability to hold at arm's length—maintaining a sense of touch but with some psychological distance; otherwise you can get swallowed up in the emotion of the moment. You need to be the voice of calm and reason.

As Dr. Boyatzis says, "Great leaders are in tune with their employees—they are in synch with the people around them. They exude hope, i.e., provide a sense of something bigger in the future, a vision, and a sense that they can take action on that future." He adds, "These leaders care about people and people know it; they have *emotional self-awareness* and are *empathetic*. And, they have *mindfulness*, i.e., a sense of being aware of the environment and what surrounds them in the moment."[3]

That describes New York Mayor Rudy Giuliani running down the street to find a new command center on 9/11. As difficult as the situation was, he exuded a sense of self-control, giving those in Manhattan and the rest of the world hope that life would go on. He remained very much aware of what was happening to him and others, and he took the most direct and positive action that he could—moment by moment.

Facing the Leadership Challenge Head On

We hope we have inspired you to step up and begin the disaster planning process in your organization, focusing especially on the human component. It may take more than one attempt to break through, but the payoff can be extremely rewarding—especially when a disaster strikes. In spite of whatever crisis you may face, employees will be re-energized and will go back to work, and you'll have a continuing, vibrant business.

Keep in mind that you don't have to go it alone in the planning and preparation phase. In addition to working with colleagues, you can take advantage of the conferences, literature resources, and self-assessment instruments offered through the Society for Human Resource Management and other organizations. Check out the Resources section starting on page 133.

Action Steps

1. Prepare for the leadership role by assessing yourself and putting a development plan together to improve or enhance your capabilities.
2. Read Chapter 2, on business continuity planning, to enhance your understanding of the process.
3. Sit down and begin to jot down your thoughts on the organization of your core team and the business continuity plan.

Chapter 2

Developing a Business Continuity Plan That Addresses Human Issues

This chapter covers the following topics:
- Educating yourself about the elements of a business continuity plan
- An overview of plan requirements
- Putting the core team together
- Creating an Emergency Operations Center
- Communications planning
- The 10 most common reasons for business continuity plan failures

Introduction

Planning for unknown events that may affect the workplace is akin to developing system requirements for new software. No matter how many bright minds get together to consider all the contingencies, there will be some potential outcome that you overlooked, never dreamed of, or could not have even imagined.

First of all, you must adopt the mindset of planning for *when* you'll face a disaster, not *if*. This will help you view the planning process as a necessity to your work and business, rather than as an abstract exercise that's using up valuable time.

Second, you have to put a plan *on paper*, developing a number of worst-case scenarios along the way. What if the entire building were to burn to the ground or be destroyed in an earthquake, tornado, flood, or explosion? What if a disaster happens during rush hour? During peak business hours? After hours? How would each of these situations affect your plans? What if a disgruntled former employee or customer came armed to your offices and opened fire, killing employees and/or others? What if one or more buses, bridges, or buildings were bombed? These dreaded events occur more often than we like to acknowledge.

So when a traumatic incident occurs, what will you do to help employees and their families get to safety so they can return to work as soon as possible? Where will they return to work? Should you plan now for contingent work space? How much and at what expense? Should you book hotel rooms to house workers temporarily? Where do you start?

Luckily, many resources are available to help you put together a business continuity plan.

Overview of Requirements

To start or update your planning, first check the federal requirements for developing and implementing employee emergency plans. The Occupational Safety and Health Administration (OSHA) general industry standards are found in the Code of Federal Regulations (CFR), Title 29, Part 1910, on the OSHA website at www.osha.gov.

The more relevant sections of Part 1910, which you can download, include:

- Subpart E—Means of Egress (1910.37 and 1910.38)
- Appendix to Subpart E—Emergency Action Plans (1910.38)
- Subpart H—Hazardous Waste Operations and Response (1910.120)
- Subpart K—Medical and First Aid (1910.151)
- Subpart L—Fire Protection (1910.155–1910.165)
- Subpart Z—Toxic and Hazardous Substances (1910.1200)

The Federal Emergency Management Agency (FEMA) offers a standardized format for planning at www.fema.gov/library/bizindex.shtm. We have provided an abbreviated outline of points to consider in the Resources section starting on page 141.

States and industries also may have special standards; for example, California has a mandatory illness and injury prevention program. Your local OSHA office should have the information you need.

In the aftermath of 9/11, many books, packaged outlines, and other resources on the topic of disaster preparedness have been made available. Be aware, however, that most of these reference materials do not cover the human elements of such planning, at least not to the extent addressed here.

What's in a Name?

Emergency preparedness, disaster recovery planning, emergency response, business resumption planning, and business continuity planning are all commonly used names for the same basic process. We use the term "business continuity planning" (BCP) in this book because it's short, it's to the point, and it implies the combination of business and people issues that is at the heart of our message. Here is a glossary of other terms that we use in this book:

- *Catastrophe:* Any great and sudden calamity or misfortune; a violent, usually destructive natural event, such as a hurricane or major earthquake; a disastrous end or outcome. Recovery usually takes a long period of time, with an end date that fluctuates or is difficult to identify.
- *Crisis:* A time of great danger or disturbance whose management determines the likelihood of negative consequences; a decisive or crucial period, stage, or event, such as a financial debacle, civil disturbance, or death of a CEO. An end date may or may not be identifiable.
- *Disaster:* A sudden event bringing great damage, loss, or destruction; an incident that is ruinous to an undertaking, such as a fire, explosion, or terrorist attack.
- *Emergency:* A sudden, unforeseen situation that requires immediate action (e.g., chemical spill or injury); an urgent need for assistance or relief, usually of short duration.
- *Emergency preparedness:* Advance planning to mitigate the adverse effects of an emergency or other unexpected occurrence.
- *Event:* A noteworthy, one-off happening that can be resolved in a short period of time.
- *Incident:* An occurrence that can be of either short or long duration.

Planning Considerations

Small companies (<300 employees)	Larger companies (≥300 employees)
Planning and disaster teams will be smaller, and the members who participate may have to play more than one role.	Planning and disaster teams will be larger and more complex. People will play specific roles, as there are more managerial resources from which to draw. Business processes and functions may also be more complex.
Plans may be less complex due to the smaller size of the business and workforce.	Plans may involve more steps and sub-steps.
Most important steps: 1. Have a plan that you follow, including some form of Incident Commander and an Emergency Operations Center. 2. Notify employees to take appropriate action based on the situation. 3. Communicate and coordinate with emergency responders. 4. Evacuate or use shelter in place. 5. Control/contain the incident. 6. Communicate with customers. 7. Protect property and records. 8. Terminate the Incident Command system and return control to management. 9. Restore normal business operations.	Same steps as for small company, with the possibility of more sub-steps given the scope of the operation and the geographic area.

Your Business Continuity Planning Team

The first decision to be made in forming the planning team is how many people to assign to it. For the initial planning and the periodic review and practice, the bigger the better. For managing the details as well as the team, a core team can be assembled. The roles and responsibilities for the core team are listed in Chapter 1.

The team that puts together the detailed plans should include representatives from all major functions in the organization, such as operations from all of the business units, engineering, finance, research and development, manufacturing, marketing, and IT. Also, if your company is organized based on geography, make sure that representatives from all of the geographic divisions are included; or require that each location develop its own business continuity plan, involving individuals from all of the relevant functions at that location. If some organizational services are centralized, such as HR and communications, make sure that the local planning group has access to those specialized resources.

The core team should include members from the following divisions:

- Human Resources
- Operations (if applicable); this person may be the Incident Commander
- Safety or security; could be ad hoc member
- Communications (or PR)

An HR executive should be designated to lead the core team and the overall planning team. The reasons are threefold:

1. HR already works with all of the major functions in the organization.
2. HR will have the most holistic perspective.
3. The HR influence will ensure that the plan deals with the human issues, not just the mechanics.

Ideally, the CEO will appoint the core team members as well as the rest of the planning team members, and give the team the power to design the plan as they see fit.

Experts to Complement Your Planning Team

As you develop, fine-tune, and try out your plan, you may want to seek counsel from resource experts. This is especially important if none of the team members has personally experienced a major disaster. It is essential that the planning be grounded in reality rather than theory.

Chapters of the American Red Cross are ready to help. Professionals from your Employee Assistance Program (EAP) or Behavioral Health Management resources can advise you or review your plan. Your local chapter of the Society for Human Resource Management (SHRM) may have a list of resources, as may your local Chamber of Commerce. Also check out the Resources section starting on page 133.

Also consider asking trusted individuals, both inside and outside your organization, who are known for their active imaginations and creative thinking to get involved in various aspects of the planning. For example, they can help you challenge your assumptions, imagine and plan scenarios (or review the scenarios you've already developed), and vet your work to date. Their different perspectives can help you build a more comprehensive plan.

The Urgency of Planning

Advance planning may be countercultural in your organization. The CEO, possibly along with the board of directors, must make it clear that such planning is a top priority; not only may lives be at stake, but the business itself could perish. If there is resistance at the top, put together a business case showing the risks and benefits of a plan. It all boils down to basic risk management and protecting your profitability. (Ideas for putting together a business case are presented in Chapter 1, in the discussion of the role of the CFO.)

It is in the shareholders' interests as well as those of employees and customers to take the time now to plan; the organization will reap multiple benefits should the plan need to be put to use. Your initial goal is to put a planning team in place and put them to work.

Dealing with Pushback

What if your leadership team claims you're acting like Chicken Little? The sky is not falling, and your organization doesn't need to take the time to prepare for a disaster that's not going to happen. Here's what you can say and do to respond.

- Recent experience shows that a number of organizations have faced disasters outside of their control, thanks to Mother Nature, such as hurricanes, tsunamis, tornadoes, floods, fires, and earthquakes. Your headquarters may not be located in a hurricane zone or tornado alley, but if your company has multiple offices, there's a good chance that one of them lies in a danger area. Share some of the recent statistics on natural disasters with the team. Also, explain that those organizations that have prepared for the worst can recover more quickly. This is not about being a company with a warm, fuzzy soul; this is about protecting the viability of the business.

- Your role is to help mitigate risks for the organization. You need to quantify what the risks would be if the organization had to shut down operations from two or three days to up to two weeks if an unforeseen event were to force employees out of work. The cost of ceasing operations and the potential cost of losing customers generally greatly exceed the out-of-pocket costs of planning and preparing. Chapter 9 provides some tips on figuring out the return on investment for a business continuity plan.

- Developing the business continuity plan, especially the first draft, involves primarily soft dollar costs in the form of staff time. This initial time investment can provide a big payoff when a disaster strikes and you need to implement your plan. And even if a disaster doesn't happen on your watch, the planning you undertake can expose a number of vulnerabilities that, if addressed, will strengthen your organization. So at a minimum, take the time to plan. Then try to get support for funding the next stages of the plan, such as setting up an Emergency Operations Center and obtaining equipment, such as battery-operated radios, satellite telephones, and backup systems.

Developing the Plan

The business continuity planning team must view the effort to develop the plan as a serious, if not critical, business project. The team must:

- Set goals, schedules, and deadlines
- Assign standard meeting times for review
- Assign specific project tasks and require periodic written reports and presentations to be submitted to the senior leadership team

Yes, employees may view their participation on this team as volunteer work in addition to their day-to-day-jobs, but they need to understand that it's crucial work that everyone must tackle and not put off. If need be, include the duties in their position/job descriptions. This is not make-work.

Team members should work both independently and collectively. From an individual perspective, representatives need to determine how their respective functions must prepare, and what they need to do to keep their departments productive and the business running in case of an emergency. In gathering the relevant data, each functional team member must analyze current business capabilities, environmental and business hazards, and the vulnerabilities of company operations and internal systems.

Collectively, the team needs to pull all of the data together and discuss it. With all of the major functions represented, the scope of thinking will be broader and the chances for a quick resumption of business will be greater.

During the discussions, be sure to cover such human issues as employee safety concerns; emergency contact information (local and outside the area); evacuation of employees, especially disabled employees; the need for trauma counseling under a variety of scenarios; workers' compensation issues; and contingent HR policies such as payroll, hazard pay for those employees working in treacherous conditions, possible benefits continuation for displaced workers, transportation to and from work, leaves of absence, and housing.

Also, consider how you will communicate with each other and with all of the other employees if telecommunications systems go down, including the company e-mail system and phone lines. Who should have satellite phones? What about cell phones with text messaging capability? Who within the company should have a personal e-mail account with a provider such as Yahoo, Microsoft, Google, and others that may be up if your systems go down? How do you share those e-mail addresses? Do you also set up group accounts and/or bulletin boards?

You also should review your business continuity plan in conjunction with your organization's other crisis-related plans. For example, your organization is likely to have developed a special crisis communication plan that covers a myriad of possible events, including product tampering, theft of intellectual or proprietary information, hostile takeover attempts, and so on. Some of the same triggers that set off the crisis communication plan will also activate the business continuity plan. It's important to make sure that you'll work in tandem rather than at cross purposes when a disaster strikes.

Team Operations: Planning versus Dealing with a Disaster

Throughout the planning process, the team can operate in any way it chooses, provided the team leader and members agree. For example, a self-organized work team approach can work quite well, if that fits your corporate culture. However, regardless of the team structure you adopt for the planning phase, you will need to establish a command-and-control structure for managing a disaster.

As anyone who has experienced a major disaster will tell you, the old-fashioned military "command and control" style, with clearly defined authority and responsibilities, is best suited for running operations during a disaster. Joe Bagan, Senior Vice President of the Southeast Region of Adelphia Communications, says that his team moves from consensus-style discussion and planning to an autocratic structure 24 hours before a hurricane is expected to touch land. The team stays in that mode for at least two to three weeks afterward. Having experienced 14 hurricanes in two years in his territory, which covers Florida, the Carolinas, and Mississippi, Bagan said he and his team are able to execute their plans quickly.

The Role of Employees

Veteran Incident Commander Jack Armstrong recommends that two or three lower-level employees participate in planning for what the organization is to do with, for, and to its workforce. This can increase employee buy-in and commitment to the process.

Creating an Emergency Operations Center

As part of business continuity planning, consider setting up a place from which to operate your business in case your premises are destroyed. Common names for such a site are Emergency Operations Center (EOC) and Disaster Recovery Site (DRS). Whatever you call it, the site should be equipped with backup computers, phones, desks, emergency supplies, and whatever else is necessary to carry on business in the short term, until new quarters can be found. Considerations include:

- *Location.* A locale some distance from the disaster may be the best choice. But it should be in an area that your employees can reach with reasonable adjustments to their commutes.

- *Space.* How many square feet will you need? Will the facility be on a different power grid? Will you need backup power?

- *Equipment.* How many phone lines, computer hookups, and intranet and Internet connections will you need? What about TV sets and radios, especially those that are battery-operated? Do you need two-way radios, walkie-talkies, satellite phones, and/or extra cell phones and pagers?

- *Staffing.* Who will be assigned to work there? What will their roles be? Make sure the roles and responsibilities of each person assigned to the EOC are crisp and clear. Who will be the Incident Commander, and how much authority will that person have? Who will make what decisions? Who will be on each shift so that there is 24-hour coverage? Who will link with fire, police, public works, state, and federal officials? Who will issue instructions for other employees to follow?

- *Reporting in.* When do employees report in to this site? How will they get there? If they are working elsewhere, how do they know where to go?

> ### Emergency Operations Center Resources
>
> Consider these supplies for your EOC:
> - Communications equipment
> - A copy of the emergency management plan and EOC procedures
> - Blueprints, maps, status boards
> - A list of EOC personnel and descriptions of their duties
> - Technical information and data for advising responders
> - Building security system information
> - Information and data management capabilities
> - Telephone directories
> - Backup power, communications, and lighting
> - Emergency supplies

How Many Business Continuity Plans Do You Need?

If your organization has just one location, one business continuity plan will probably suffice. However, if you have multiple locations or even occupy several floors in a single high-rise, you may want to consider developing separate plans for each unit, department, or location. You also may need more than one Emergency Operations Center depending on how spread out you are.

For example, a university, hospital, or company campus that has many buildings with different functions may need a unit-level plan, because the entire population may not face a threat of the same urgency as those employees in the building or area where the emergency occurs. For example, if a lone gunman enters a building and opens fire, the *immediate* impact will be on the employees in the general vicinity. Their lives, safety, and security are the ones initially at stake. Your plan needs to address that.

Components of Emergency Response

A major part of any business continuity plan is determining how to respond when an emergency rises. There are at least 10 components to an emergency response. These conform to the OSHA requirements in CFR Part 1910, Subparts 38 and 39, *Emergency Action Plans* and *Fire Prevention Plans*:

- Make sure that the EOC management team members know their own responsibilities and duties in the event of an emergency and what staff members are assigned to them. It makes sense to think about management structure in the context of how and where it will be used.

- Think through the role of Incident Commander very carefully. This individual will run the show in any event that requires you to open the EOC. A good choice to fill this role might be the VP of operations, the chief operating officer, or the plant manager. Sufficient operating authority must be delegated to enable this person to make decisions on the run, without having to crawl up the chain of command, which may become broken. The Incident Commander should have a team of people who also are able to make significant decisions.

- Establish duties for crucial employees. This group includes anyone who is required to handle critical operations during and immediately after an evacuation—shutting down equipment, for example.

- Establish procedures for reporting fires and other emergencies.

- Identify contacts. Which outside agencies and internal personnel should be notified in case of an emergency? Who will contact them?

- Identify evacuation schemes to use in emergency situations. Escape procedures should include floor plans and workplace maps showing where refuge areas are located.

- Establish a procedure to account for all employees after an evacuation has been executed, or even after a disaster. Besides the traditional phone tree of home numbers, consider the use of cell phones, especially those with text messaging.

- Install alarm and communications systems.

- Develop and implement requirements and methods for training managers, employees, and emergency response teams.
- Keep records during and after an emergency or disaster.
- Review your plan periodically and update it, if necessary.

Practicing Emergency Response

Being prepared is the first requirement for responding effectively to an emergency. But preparation alone won't prevent you from becoming fearful or yielding to the impulse to flee when disaster strikes. Fear and flight are instinctual, compelling reactions, even among professionals such as firefighters and police, who have undergone extensive training in crisis response.

To counter this natural impulse, Larry Parsons, Director of Environmental Health and Safety at the University of California at Santa Barbara, insists on drilling for various types of emergencies. He calls on the business continuity team members and others to act out the roles they will play in a crisis. Those who don't have a specific role practice evacuating the site. Practice can reduce panic because individuals know that they have specific duties to perform or places to go. Build realistic simulations into your plan.

Considering Employees

Any time a disaster strikes, the first priority is the safety of employees. Three critical questions must be answered:

- **Where is everyone?** Generally, HR activates the telephone tree, and managers of various departments and locations check on the whereabouts of their staff members. Depending on the type of emergency and the time of day it happened, you may need to call employees' home numbers or cell phones or perhaps send text messages.
- **Are employees safe?** Are there any injuries or fatalities? If so, you'll need to activate the injury or fatality response portion of your plan.
- **Do employees have the basics?** Do they have a roof over their heads? Water? Food? Clothing? Family members or pets with them—or do they at least know where their family members and pets are? If they haven't had these basic needs

addressed, they will have a difficult time concentrating on their work—if they in fact show up to work.

"The reason you're helping employees with their self-preservation is not empathy or compassion, but a bottom-line business reason," explains Charles Pizzo. "You need your employees to come back to work to get the business going. If they don't come back to work, you're not going to be able to recover."

In addition to following up on employees, you also have to check in with your senior leaders to assess how they're coping. Some senior executives may be in a state of panic and unable to function. In such a situation, the HR leader needs to step up as an example and remain as dispassionate as possible.

It is the HR leader's responsibility to be the voice of reason and calm. Even if the CEO is managing well, you should expect that he or she will look to you as the HR representative for counsel, especially on internal matters concerning employees. You represent a center or safe haven for all employees based on your self-control, the ability to "touch" at arm's length, and the determination to inspire confidence and take command. You cannot wait to be asked—just do.

Veteran Incident Commander Jack Armstrong says, "Manage your emotional side as you take control of the situation. If you act like you are in control, then you *become* in control."

You also will need to activate the contingent HR policies you've developed. Because you have prepared them in advance as part of the business continuity planning process, you won't have to scramble when disaster strikes. You may need to adjust these policies to fit the specific situation you face, but that's a lot easier than creating them from scratch under stress.

Planning for Timely Business Resumption

Once you have verified that your employees are in a safe zone, the next critical step is to make sure that the business continues to run as smoothly as possible, given the circumstances. Important decisions that must be made—ideally, when you are still in the process of preparing your business continuity plan—include the following:

- Decide where the business will be relocated in case your premises must be evacuated for a lengthy period. This may or may not be the same site as the Emergency Operations Center.
- Determine who will make the call to activate the EOC, and specify which operating and support units will relocate there.
- Determine, if necessary, what housing arrangements will be required for transferred staff and how they will be paid for.
- Establish a system for emergency funding, backup check writing, and other banking processes.
- Plan for the activation of backup systems and/or the ability to access outsourced systems. There are enormous issues facing the information technology (IT) leaders in contingent planning, including the locations of hardware and backup software, the availability of contingent resources, the provision of backup copies of systems documentation and operating instructions, details of equipment replacement, and a list of the names of outside resources and specialists. Also allow for a backup telephone system.
- Plan for the backup and transfer of electronic records.
- Analyze paper files and determine which records can be transferred to electronic files. Imagine how, if all files should disappear, the business would run without them. At First Interstate Bank the HR files were damaged by smoke in a major fire. Our options were to clean the documents or toss them. We tossed most of them. In New Orleans and other cities ravaged by the 2005 hurricanes, complete buildings were ruined and all their contents lost. While you may not be in hurricane territory, disasters such as building fires or floods can occur, so plan accordingly.
- Determine which records should be transferred to the recovery site.
- Determine which computer files need to be backed up and arrange in advance for their off-site storage, maintenance, and updating.
- Determine the procedure for verifying where staff members are working. Establish contingent policies to cover disruptions such as the inability to use public transportation and longer commute times.

- Identify ways to notify customers of changes in operations and what it means to them.
- Redirect leadership to the EOC.
- Evaluate control and financial risks for each major business and support function—for example, backup payroll, pension/401(k) reporting, and administration for HR.

Ensuring the Success of Your Plan

Although your plan must cover many topics, you should strive to keep the execution portion as simple as possible. Focus on *what* people need to do, in what order. Keeping the plan as simple as possible will make it easier for the team to carry it out and for employees to understand what to do. Documents and supporting materials such as handouts and wall posters should be written in plain, easy-to-read language. This is not the time for legalese or military-style requirements. Observe the KISS principle—*keep it sweet and simple.*

Make sure that people in several locations on each floor and in all buildings and locations of the business have assigned roles and know how to carry them out in case of an emergency. The greater the number of people who are involved, the more buy-in and commitment there will be to the plan.

Practice, Practice, Practice

Practice carrying out the plan, preferably at least twice a year. Keep the sessions interesting and different so that employees are forced to pay attention. Include role playing under various disaster scenarios. Also, participate in any disaster exercises sponsored by local emergency planning agencies. And above all, take the exercises seriously. As mentioned earlier, practice helps reduce fear; when employees at all levels know what they are supposed to do, they are better able to resist the urge to simply flee.

Dr. Mory Framer, an expert in dealing with trauma, says,

> In scenario planning you may try to conceive of every possible situation, but the one you haven't prepared for will be the one that happens. Don't be surprised if you are surprised. Plan and carry out practice exercises. Think about what you're learning when you do them.

Be prepared for "open field running"; that is, the play called out by the quarterback in the huddle may not be the one that is executed after the ball is thrown. Players make quick decisions on the run.

He adds, "Things don't always go the way you plan, but emergencies and disasters have the same patterns, and the same lessons will apply. That's why preparation and practice are so important. Keep your eyes open. This is fundamental, and it's what allows you to make changes on the run."

Do You Practice in the Dark?

Are you practicing your simulations without electrical power and without landline telephone service? That's a great way to test the thoroughness of your plan, as well as your ability to handle a severe situation.

Charles Pizzo, a 20-year communications veteran, crisis communications expert, and Hurricane Katrina evacuee, says you don't have a true emergency preparedness plan until you test it in the absence of electricity and landline and cell phone service.

As he points out, it's rare to face a complete collapse of the telecommunications structure, as New Orleans experienced with Hurricane Katrina. In fact, there's no comparable word for "blackout" to describe the complete shutdown of the telephone system. Yet it did happen—and it could happen again.

Joe Bagan, Senior Vice President of the Southeast Region of Adelphia Communications, echoes Pizzo's assertion. "People don't grasp how dependent we are on power. It's hard to fathom all the things you can't do without power and all the things that can break down. For instance, you can't get gasoline, so you can't drive to the grocery store, to work, to the hospital, and to wherever else you need to go."

Communicating with Employees

As mentioned earlier, your business continuity plan requires a component that addresses how you will communicate with employees before, during, and after a disaster. Major issues to consider include the following.

Before a Disaster

Regularly communicate the importance of disaster planning and preparation for the business and for individuals. Share the key components of your business continuity plan, including what actions employees will need to take if disaster strikes. (Basics include how to evacuate the building, whom to call for further instructions, and whom to notify if there is a problem.)

Also, encourage employees to make plans for themselves and their families, independent of what's happening at work, including getting supplies. Refer them to the excellent resource materials available from the Red Cross and other agencies. You don't have to re-create materials. You do have to reinforce employees' knowledge of the actions they need to take at work to reach safety—or, if disaster strikes during off hours, how they are to get in touch with their managers to make sure they're accounted for. See "Suggested Actions to Take at Home" in the Resources section on page 157.

You also need to get to know representatives of the local media—especially those in radio news—in the cities and towns where you have offices, plants, and other operations. Depending on the severity of the disaster, you may need the help of local radio and TV stations—those that still have their own news departments—to broadcast messages. Ideally, you always want to communicate directly with employees, but that may not be possible. The news media usually will cooperate, especially if you're a major employer in their market, as they will thereby be providing a public service duty as well as reporting breaking news. For example, they can broadcast a special toll-free number for employees, which you should have set up in advance, as well as a special website, which also should be prepared in advance.

Also, for all the communications team members and those involved with business continuity, set up personal e-mail accounts with such providers as Yahoo, Microsoft, and Google. That way if your organization's e-mail system goes down but Internet service is still available, you'll be able to communicate with each other. You also may want to encourage employees to share their personal e-mail addresses with their managers for the telephone tree.

During the Disaster

Communicate often in as many ways as you can, considering the tools you have available. The initial messages should focus on the safety of employees and their families in the disaster area, and all the "me" issues, such as:

- Do I come to work?
- Where?
- When?
- What's happening to my benefits?
- What about filing insurance claims for damage to my home? Can I take time off from work for that?

Be sure to communicate to employees in unaffected areas too. They'll want to know what's happening with their co-workers, and what they can do to help. For example, can they prepare and send care packages? Can they give blood? Are cash donations better? Later, they'll need to know how their job duties may change—for example, if they need to cover for certain people or tasks, or if they'll be working with more employees if you decide to relocate employees to unaffected areas and offices.

For affected and unaffected employees, there's a very good chance that you won't know all the answers to all the questions in advance. However, you can say, "We don't know. We're looking into it, and we'll get back to you," and then do so. See the Prologue for real-life examples.

Once you address these basic needs, you can start communicating what's happening with the business, including the plans for recovery.

Also, as soon as it's safe, have your leaders meet face to face with employees. Group meetings, especially when people can see their co-workers en masse, can be therapeutic experiences. You're survivors! These meetings are also good opportunities to assess in real time how well your overall business continuity plan is working from the employees' perspective, as well as the employee communication portion, and what changes you need to make on the fly. Also, employees appreciate seeing their leaders on the front line rather than hiding out in a bunker somewhere.

After the Disaster

Once your business is back on track, you need to balance two types of communications: the follow-up messages related to the disaster and the ongoing business messages. To put it another way: You want to be respectful of what has happened, especially if some employees and their families have suffered, but you don't want to get stuck in the past. If you don't watch it, you risk encouraging everyone to relive their experiences. The employees and the organization both have to move on.

Keep in mind that you may have some employees who remain traumatized, and it is important *not* to say "Get on with it" when they are not emotionally ready. Keep the trauma consultants handy just in case. Those affected employees also need to be counseled carefully by the managers so that they can return to productive work as soon as possible, as discussed in the following chapters.

For everyone, however, it can be a healing exercise to document for employees, their families, and the organization what happened. This communication, especially if it's print or video, can serve as a record of events that pays tribute to a challenging time and that recognizes people for their efforts.

For example, in September 2002 Agilent Technologies issued on its intranet a special series remembering 9/11 and reminding employees about the importance of disaster preparedness. The series featured personal perspectives from three employees who assisted the rescue efforts using Agilent technology, and reviewed the actions Agilent leaders took to ensure the safety of employees. There were also wellness tips for dealing with traumatic events, and a checklist of how to be prepared amidst the potential confusion of an emergency situation.

However, you also have to focus on events happening now and those on the horizon, especially if the competitive landscape has changed. For example, competitors may be providing products and services your customers need but can't get from your organization at present. Therefore, you need to work with your company leaders to refocus, re-engage, and re-energize employees.

10 Common Mistakes

Even though you have put considerable effort into emergency preparedness, things can still go badly when disaster strikes. However, adverse consequences can be minimized if you avoid the following pitfalls:

1. *No senior management support.* A well-known health care company that was suffering financial reverses decided to cut the budgets for training and emergency preparedness. The company was ill prepared for the problems it then faced as a result of September 11. Although it is common for training to be cut when budgets have to be trimmed severely, CEOs and CFOs should think twice about the cost of not being prepared to serve customers in case of a disaster and weigh that cost against the small amount of savings derived from cutting the costs of maintaining emergency preparedness.

2. *Lack of employee buy-in.* A typical employee reaction might be "Oh, yeah, another stupid fire drill." But it's not stupid; in fact, it is necessary for saving lives. Change the drill and change employees' roles so that they know what is expected of every emergency

response team member and what could happen if they aren't prepared.

3. *Insufficient planning.* This should not be a problem if you solicit the input of key employees across a broad spectrum of departments and get their help in fleshing out the plan and updating it regularly.

4. *Lack of training and practice.* Make exercises interesting; run them often enough that employees learn something new each time. Include the training as part of new-employee orientation programs. (Also, certain states require annual safety training. Find out if yours does.)

5. *No designated leader.* Leadership is key. Make sure that an Incident Commander is appointed and that team leadership roles are well defined. Offer leadership training when necessary. If you're in a hurricane zone, you may want to consider rotating the Incident Commander role so that you won't burn out your leaders.

6. *Failure to keep the plan up to date.* This plan should not be the type that goes in a three-ring binder and is immediately forgotten. Make it part of regular safety training for all employees, and update names, phone numbers, and agency contacts as often as necessary. (Maintenance of the plan could be a good project for a high-potential person.)

7. *No method for alerting employees.* Everyone should know the key people to call in order to sound an alert and whom or where to call for information. Create a telephone tree in the form of a simple card to carry in a wallet or purse or to keep next to the telephone at home; make it available to be entered in a laptop or PDA. Do not give this detail short shrift! A sample wallet card is provided on page 145 in the Resources section. Or include an emergency telephone number on each employee's ID card.

8. *OSHA regulations not part of the plan.* The design we are recommending is based on OSHA regulations. Do not let your eyes glaze over at the thought of reading regulations; the Code of Federal Regulations is not so daunting. Become familiar with it. Read the many booklets provided by the Federal Emergency Management Agency and OSHA. They are thorough and will prove very helpful in your planning.

9. *No procedures for shutting down critical equipment.* Who turns out the lights? Who turns off the generators, gas lines, or turbine engines? How do they do it and when, and who will give final instructions for this?
10. *Employees not told what actions to take in an emergency.* Employee communications *must* be a linchpin of your plan.

Action Steps

1. Do the basic research on federal regulations. Visit the FEMA website and either download their manual or order a hardcopy. Your local Red Cross office may have copies in stock.
2. Organize the strategic core team and the tactical core team, defining roles and responsibilities, with careful selection of who should be on each team.
3. Kick off the planning processes.
4. Spend time determining how to establish an Emergency Operations center (EOC), where it could be located, and how it would be furnished.
5. Be sure to define the roles and responsibilities of each person who is delegated to move to the EOC in case of a disaster.
6. Be sure all people issues are covered in the plan.
7. Practice, practice, practice your scenarios!
8. Ensure that communications staff do communication planning, including developing key messages and key template materials in advance of their need.
9. Make sure your plan avoids the 10 common mistakes that cause business continuity plans to fail.

Chapter 3

Creating Contingent HR Policies

This chapter focuses on three areas:
- Your organization's philosophy for the treatment of employees in general and contingencies for a disaster in specific
- Subjects for which you may want to establish contingent Human Resources policies
- Planning for emergency employee communications

Philosophy on Interim Human Resource Management

Some organizations develop an overarching Human Resources philosophy that fits their vision or mission. It goes beyond the "Employees are our most precious asset" cliché; it states how you value your workforce and how you exemplify that value through the types of Human Resources programs and policies you establish.

You need to take this philosophy into account when you start your business continuity planning. Your philosophy should be the underpinning of your plan. We also strongly recommend your plan include contingent policies for dealing with HR issues, and that these policies align with the plan and with your HR philosophy.

When developing contingent policies, the business continuity planning team, or a subteam, should discuss with senior leaders the organization's values as they relate to the treatment of people during times of crisis. These contingent policies, which also should include how you wish to treat your customers and their demands, will serve to support the business and will be especially helpful in achieving a speedy and efficient business recovery.

Establishing contingent Human Resources policies in advance of a disaster is similar to investing in a thermostat rather than just a thermometer. With a thermostat, you're not just measuring temperature; you're also realizing the ability to control and change the temperature quickly. By having contingent policies already present in your business continuity plan, you are able to quickly switch to a new way of operating that suits the situation. You'll save valuable time in addition to restoring employees' confidence that their leaders are taking charge and considering issues that are of top priority to employees: "What about me? How is this disaster affecting my personal finances?"

Neither the planning team nor HR can afford to develop the policies in a vacuum; all must agree on how the organization wishes to care for its employees in times of duress and emotional pain. You don't want to be second-guessed later or run the risk of inconsistent compliance, which can breed resentment among employees. Depending on the situation that ensues, you may need to alter your policies at a moment's notice to fit the circumstances, but at least you'll have a philosophical base from which to work.

Basic HR Policies

The basic policies to consider are those for meeting employees' immediate needs once they and their families are safe: policies surrounding pay and benefits and the return to work.

Paychecks

How will you physically pay employees, especially if they've relocated and do not use direct deposit? Can you give pay statements and checks to managers at specified delivery locations announced by the control center? Or do you set up a conveniently located pickup center (or centers)? Managers or someone in the control center should take the responsibility for ensuring that employees receive their pay statements or checks in a timely fashion. So that you will be able to cut and deposit checks, be sure to develop backup and contingency plans for payroll processing, including delivery of statements and checks.

You could lose all your records in a flood, hurricane, or fire, so plan ahead. If you use an outside payroll service, plan for the ability to recapture input and uploads so that you can pay people as quickly as possible according to your schedule. If you do your own payroll processing, give serious thought to your means of data capture and backup so that all will not be lost in case your computers, disks, servers, and the like become unusable. Pay becomes even more precious to employees who face the prospect of losing it all, as we saw with the Gulf Coast hurricanes during the fall of 2005.

Employee Wages

Continuation of employee wages is one of the most significant items to plan for in advance. To what extent will you pay people if they are not able to work for a period of time? Employees whose work is exempt from overtime provisions under federal and state wage regulations are normally paid a salary irrespective of the hours worked. That's generally fine if the power goes out for a day, but what if the power is out for three weeks or more, and there is no place for employees to report to work, conditions that many businesses experienced in the aftermath of Hurricane Katrina?

What's your philosophy on continuation of wages? How long can you afford to pay not only exempt employees, but hourly workers as well? Make these decisions now as part of your business continuity plan, so that when something serious happens, you can quickly get the word out to employees. For example, you may want to set a policy for a few days of continued pay. Once disaster strikes and you have a better feel for the length of the disruption, you can make a more informed decision and go back and tell your people what you're doing about their pay. Don't promise to pay them for X period of time and then renege on that; start low and go higher, not the other way around.

In your planning, you should consider alternative pay arrangements that fit your industry as well as your budget. Examples might include continuing to pay employees who are unable to report to work because the state or local government has closed the roads, or those who, due to other transportation problems, cannot physically get to work or to an alternative work location.

You might also give employees the option to use vacation time or days from their "paid time off" bank, even if the use of such time generally requires people to give advance notice.

Hazard Pay

As part of your business continuity planning, think about the extent to which you will need employees to come back to work as soon as possible to restore key products or services to the public, such as power, phones, cable, health care, or gasoline, or to meet customer needs. Will you need to provide hazard pay to acknowledge that these people may be risking their lives to enter and work in a danger zone? Will you need to increase this hazard pay during the course of the hurricane season to encourage and reward those who volunteer to work key shifts? And to what degree do overtime pay and hazard pay count toward employee benefits, such as life insurance and 401(k) contributions?

For example, Joe Bagan of the cable company Adelphia Communications said that management decided to increase its hazard pay during the 2005 hurricane season. Initially, people were willing to volunteer both for altruistic reasons and to earn more money. But as the season wore on and workers grew tired, the organization determined it should provide greater incentives for employees to work longer hours in difficult situations.

Regardless of your philosophy and decisions, you need to notify employees as quickly as possible as to how you plan to manage their pay during the disaster or emergency period.

Finally, if you require employees to continue working (or make a special plea for them to continue), we recommend you not only consider providing them with regular pay, overtime pay as earned, and hazardous-duty pay, but also plan on reimbursing all reasonable expenses, such as transportation and any extra costs employees may incur because of the situation.

Continuation of Benefits

You also need to think about how employees will use their benefits, especially their health care, during an emergency or disaster. What if employees need medical treatment but can't easily get to a network provider or obtain the proper advance authorizations? What if employees don't have their medical ID cards with them?

What if they're stuck at a worksite without their prescription medicines? What if an employee's eyeglasses break or become lost?

HR needs to work with health care providers and administrators to develop procedures for cutting through the red tape to get employees the medical care they need while protecting the company's financial investments.

Timekeeping

If timekeeping is important in your organization, managers—or others—must assume responsibility for ensuring that employees properly record their work hours. If you change payroll distribution sites, you'll need to announce the new locations for picking up and delivering timekeeping materials. You should also plan for any special accounting that may be necessary for insurance claim purposes. This generally will require its own documentation.

Work Reassignment

Depending on the situation, you may need to reassign work roles. Employees should be alerted to the new roles as soon as possible. In some cases, you may need to request that employees remain available during regular working hours so they can report to work immediately once you are ready to resume operations.

If you reassign staff to other duties or locations, try to make sure the commuting distance is reasonable. And you should be sensitive to family situations, such as employees needing to find alternative day care services for children, making arrangements for elder care, or attending to other personal business that may interfere with their work—if they are able to get to work.

In extreme situations—such as Hurricane Katrina, in which large communities and entire towns were displaced—major employers such as Wal-Mart encouraged and assisted in the relocation of employees so that they could take jobs at other company locations across the country.

Employee Assistance and Behavioral Health Programs

Most HR crisis veterans will agree that that the area of employee assistance and behavioral health requires planning; expertise, often from outside professionals; and investment. Leaders and employees, especially those who have never experienced a disaster, may think they can go it alone both personally and at their jobs without professional help. However, it's best to mitigate both short- and long-term risks by making such help available. The later chapters in this book address the value of investing in this type of care to help employees heal and return to productive work.

Returning to Work

Some disasters and emergency situations may be so traumatic that employees become apprehensive about returning to work. They worry about their physical and/or emotional safety. They don't want to re-enter the building, they don't want to ride in the elevators, and they don't want to go to certain floors. In these cases, employees have the opportunity to request a leave of absence, according to state and federal leave requirements, and this should be a part of the company's leave-of-absence policy. In addition, HR and management should direct affected employees to the Employee Assistance Program. If no EAP exists, you should consider bringing in professionals on a temporary or ad hoc basis to help employees deal with the crisis.

When an employee announces that he or she will not be returning to work, the employee's manager and the HR representative need to establish whether the employee is voluntarily resigning or should be offered a personal leave of absence. In the former case, you should establish a time frame under which a voluntary resignation would occur (such as five days after an employee fails to report to work).

In instances where an employee fears working in the building or location where the incident occurred, you should make a reasonable effort to transfer the employee. However, if the business needs require that the employee work in the building, with no alternative, the manager (or HR) has to notify the employee of the company's inability to accommodate a transfer, and of the implications. Both the manager and HR staff member should encourage the employee to use EAP resources.

Parking and Other Transportation Issues

When parking accessibility is affected by a disaster or emergency, you should quickly switch over to the parking alternatives provided for in your business continuity plan, and you should communicate the new arrangements. If employees have to pay more for parking than what they had been paying previously, try to reimburse them for their additional parking expenses.

Employees using public transportation who are unable to use their prepaid passes should continue to be reimbursed at the same rate as during normal business operations. The policy statement should limit the extent to which reimbursement continues after a designated time period.

Depending on the nature of your business and the disaster, you may want to secure alternative forms of transportation, such as vans or car services, to bring critical staff members to the company's business location.

Reimbursement for Lodging and Related Expenses

You may need to secure lodging for employees who are unable to return home following a disaster—a hotel room, apartment, or other form of temporary housing. The policy statement should establish a reasonable time frame for reimbursing expenses based on the scope of the disaster and the company's ability to pay.

Depending on your company culture, such temporary housing could include shelter in other employees' homes. Decide ahead of time, as you develop your business continuity plan, whether you want to encourage employees to open their homes to their co-workers, and also whether you want company staff to be involved in the matchmaking.

Employees who are temporarily homeless may face numerous other issues that can hinder their ability to focus on work, even when they're ready to return. For example, an employee may be separated from his or her spouse and children, who have relocated to another area temporarily; may not have work clothes; or may be hesitant to travel on business trips because of lack of appropriate clothes and a suitcase to pack them in. Also, employees may be preoccupied with the reacquisition of housing. In addition to establishing policies to address this situation, HR staff may choose to devote some time and resources to guiding these employees through the labyrinth of difficulties they face.

Other Policies

Interim policies should be developed for the following areas:

- **Flexible working hours.** Flextime can be helpful in meeting employees' personal needs and also in managing resources. For instance, employees whose daily commute time has increased significantly because of the emergency may appreciate the option of working flexible hours. Also, if managers have limited equipment and space for staff—such as one personal computer and two full-time workers who need to use it, or a lack of empty cubicles—they may choose to stagger employees' hours to accommodate short-term scheduling needs. Also, you could ask employees to work at home and avoid the pressure of finding them new space and equipment. In this situation, the manager, IT division, and HR must ensure that employees have the equipment, network access, and other resources they need to do their jobs. Also, if the manager has never supervised home workers before, he or she needs to get a brief tutorial from HR on the ins and outs of managing a remote workforce.

- **Expense reimbursement.** HR and senior leaders should determine what guidance they will give to managers and employees concerning the types of reasonable expenses that are eligible for reimbursement in an emergency. For example, will the organization pay for all cell phone calls, not just business-related ones? Will the company provide toll-free numbers that employees can use to avoid incurring toll charges? Will managers be able to provide lunches at company expense for employees who return to work quickly to start rebuilding morale? What if a manager needs to buy some business supplies? Will you authorize special expense accounts that managers and employees can use for emergency-related expenses? How will these expenses be approved?

- **Recognition.** If you have recognition policies or a special program, review it to determine how well it may be expected to work when a disaster strikes. For example, it may be geared more toward acknowledging an employee's quick thinking to save the day rather than showing appreciation for someone's lengthy dedication under trying personal and professional circumstances. Think about how you can recognize those individuals who go beyond the normal call of duty.

- **Dress code.** Give some thought to a dress code appropriate to the situation. Stuffy, formal First Interstate, for example, immediately relaxed its dress code after its building fire in order to have one less "corporate" code for employees to deal with. How important is maintaining a strict business-casual dress code when six people are trying to share one cubicle?

- **Availability of HR staff.** The HR team needs to develop procedures for HR staff to be available to both managers and employees to assist them with any issues or questions they may have. You may consider making HR staff accessible to all shifts and after hours. Then think about how to get HR staff the support they need to manage their personal lives.

- **Contributions from other employees.** Employees who aren't personally inconvenienced by the disaster may be willing to help out their co-workers. Consider the extent to which you will help employees make cash contributions, donate food and clothing, adjust their schedules to cover for employees who can't work, or give up vacation time.

Planning for Emergency Employee Communication

You should establish the capability for setting up an Emergency Operations Center (EOC) before a disaster so that it can be opened as quickly as possible. Human Resources should have access to all employee contact information, and managers should have contact information for the employees in their departments. This information should include the employee's home phone number, cell phone number, work e-mail address, personal e-mail address, home address, local emergency contact information (phone numbers, e-mail addresses, and street addresses), and out-of-area emergency contact information (phone numbers with area codes and time zones, and e-mail addresses).

You should investigate the use of both electronic and nonelectronic formats for collecting and storing this information, as well as updating it on a regular basis. Even if employees can update this information on their own through your enterprise software, remind them periodically to do so. Keep in mind that a business continuity plan is ineffective if it doesn't provide for the ability to contact employees.

Develop telephone trees or other means of contacting employees. Be aware that electronic communication will not work if the power goes out, if wiring or cell towers are compromised, or if batteries die.

As Charles Pizzo, the crisis communications expert and Hurricane Katrina evacuee, discovered when the entire telecommunications structure went down (as described on his website, www.charlespizzo.com), people had to be very clever to establish contact. They posted flyers in shelters, advertised on radio and TV, put up banners where people might see them, and posted critical information on websites for those who had left the area and had Internet access at their new locales.

Action Steps

1. Work with senior leadership team to develop a strategic HR philosophy that fits and advances the organization's vision, mission, and key business strategies. The philosophy should encompass the ways in which the organization plans to:
   a. Recruit, select, hire, and develop its people
   b. Pay and reward employees
   c. Provide care, such as benefits
   d. Create a positive and productive workplace through the culture and organizational climate it hopes to achieve
   e. Recognize employees for heroic actions
   f. Coach, counsel, discipline, and terminate employees who are characterized by poor performance

2. Determine in advance, in the course of business continuity planning, how you will use this philosophy to address employee issues such as the following:
   a. Pay
   b. Attendance
   c. Trauma
   d. Benefits
3. Work with communications staff to develop ways to convey these contingent HR policies to employees.

Part II

Dealing with Disasters

The information in this section forms the guts of how to respond when you are faced with a disaster, small or large: what to do when a disaster is unfolding, as you move through the aftermath, and as you work through the longer-term recovery period. These chapters cover the following topics:

- How to help employees at all levels deal with their emotional reactions to a sudden shift in the business equilibrium: fear, anger, shock, depression, guilt, sadness, or one or more other feelings. You'll find a recounting of what one company did when an employee murdered seven of his fellow employees and how the company worked quickly to address the resulting trauma and to involve the affected employees in designing their healing process.

- How to train HR staff, managers, risk managers, and communications staff to prepare them to help their affected colleagues, and to protect the business as well.

- How to balance the needs of employees in the aftermath of a disaster with those of the business, including tips and tools for speeding up the business recovery.

- How to get yourself back to functioning effectively in the aftermath so that you can deal with employees and their needs.

- Gaining an understanding of the emotional wear and tear on employees at all levels, and helping employees heal in a timely manner through the use of outside behavioral health professionals.
- Some ideas on problem solving that will enable you to begin the planning process now.

Chapter 4

Taking Care of Employees

This chapter covers the following topics:
- Seven steps to take immediately following a disaster to ensure that employees are safe and accounted for
- Managerial self-awareness and self-control
- Caring for employees under extreme conditions
- Tips for managing the human side of a crisis

Overview

Taking care of employees immediately after a disaster means making sure they are safe and secure. That's the overarching issue for the employees and their families. Once that's taken care of, you need to lead both purposefully and symbolically to get employees out of crisis mode and back to work. Your leadership actions will ease the employees' anxiety, help to resolve and address the ambiguity of the situation, and provide employees with a sense of purpose, direction, and hope.

Seven Critical Steps

The broad actions you must take to deal with the human side of a crisis can be condensed into these seven procedures, generally performed in this order:

1. Make sure the Incident Commander has assumed control and has started to give directions, such as ordering the opening of the Emergency Operations Center if the incident is serious enough to warrant such action.

2. Account for all employees on the premises to make sure they are safe and secure, and they are getting any needed medical care. Locate employees who were not at the disaster location to make sure they are also safe and secure, and determine if they need any help.

3. Tell employees what immediate actions you're taking and what they need to do; also inform the media as appropriate. Use whatever means you have at your disposal to contact and communicate with employees. (See Chapters 2 , 5, and 7 for suggestions.)

4. Make adjustments on the fly to respond to changes in the situation.

5. Role-model the behavior you want from employees.

6. Assess the need for trauma counseling (including screening) and, if counseling is needed, make arrangements for it.

7. Repeat this process as needed, starting with step 3.

The number of times you will repeat the seven-step process depends on the type of disaster, its scope, and the degree of trauma to which your employees are exposed. For example, in terms of the employees' safety and security, you have to deal with both reality and perception. Sometimes people perceive that they're in a safe spot but are actually in danger, as in the case of someone driving on roads with downed power lines after a storm to get to family members. At other times people perceive that they're in a danger zone, such as a person riding an elevator to an upper floor a few months after a building fire or earthquake, but in fact they're experiencing post-traumatic stress.

Also, events can unfold over the course of minutes, hours, days, weeks, or months, with frequent changes, which is another reason to keep this cycle going. The information you share with employees should consist of more than factual updates. If you provide helpful hints on managing stress and coping with issues related to the disaster, you'll be encouraging employees to regain a sense of control over their situation, which will be empowering. Included at the end of this chapter is an example of the information First Interstate provided its employees to help them deal with stress.

Modeling Self-Awareness and Self-Control

The longer a crisis continues, the harder it becomes for leaders to stay calm and confident; but they need to maintain that state, or at least project it. Self-awareness and self-control are key competencies in a crisis. If you lose your cool, you'll contribute to the confusion and make things worse. And if you shut down due to the emotional shock, you won't be able to do your job and lead.

As Joe Bagan, Southeast Region Senior Vice President for Adelphia Communications (the cable company), explained, "I work with and teach my leadership team to project confidence and calm. There's enough chaos and stress to go around. You can't look as if you've got your hair on fire. That plus any other aura signs you display in your writing, speaking, or movements will leak out and cause more disarray." It is important for a leader to keep a demeanor of professionalism—along with empathy and passion—and to serve as a role model on how to behave.

Also, regardless of your leadership style under normal conditions, you need to adopt a command-and-control management structure when disaster strikes. Taking control to the extent possible will help you stabilize the situation, minimize risks, and avoid additional problems.

Caring for Employees under Extreme Conditions

The following, true story of Edgewater Technology illustrates how company leaders quickly sprang into action when disaster struck during what was expected to be a quiet day during a slow period at work. Although Edgewater didn't have a business continuity plan (except for plans for dealing with a building fire), the company had leaders who thought on their feet, responded rapidly, and took care of their employees. This story also shows how the company involved employees in the recovery process.

An Unforeseen and Unimaginable Scenario

On Tuesday, December 26, 2000, a disgruntled employee entered the Wakefield, Massachusetts, lobby of Edgewater Technology and shot and killed the receptionist and the Director of Human Resources, who happened to be standing in the reception area. The employee gunman then walked down the hall and killed three more employees, and then went to the Accounting Department, where he took out two more. In total, seven employees lost their lives.

Minutes after the shootings, Kathleen McComber, the Vice President of Human Resources at the time, learned about the situation from news reports at her Little Rock, Arkansas, location. She immediately contacted the company CEO in Wakefield. A crisis management team was established. These individuals included the president at the Wakefield site and her senior management team, the corporate legal counsel, the corporate CFO, the corporate CEO, and McComber herself.

That afternoon the team interviewed and selected a team of Boston-area resource professionals. Because they were local, they would be familiar with local issues and could start to work immediately. The team also took on several new members, including a crisis management consultant, lawyers, crisis counselors, and a host of community supporters. The crisis team sought skills and expertise in communications, disaster recovery, law, counseling, and security.

Caring for the Victims' Families

McComber explained, "During a four-hour conference call we developed and put into action a plan to support the victims' families and our employees. The health of, support for, and communication with these two groups were our first priorities."

The crisis team assigned a member of the management group to each family affected by the shooting. This manager was to be the sole contact with the family, so that there would be only one avenue of communications and he or she would be responsible for keeping them updated about the plans. All information concerning benefits and other employee matters flowed through this person. Each manager contacted his or her assigned family on the first night and continued to communicate on a daily basis, or more frequently, if necessary, and also visited the family at home.

Caring for the Wakefield Site Employees

Immediately after the shootings, the president at the Wakefield site closed the office and sent everyone home. By Thursday, two days later, Edgewater Technology had signed up all the surviving Wakefield employees in critical-incident support therapy at an off-site location. These sessions lasted about two hours. The group sessions continued for several days. The company made available one-on-one counseling sessions as well.

The crisis team also set up an employee hotline and contacted as many people as possible via e-mail, telephone, and personal visits. Because it was the holiday season, many employees were away. Nonetheless, the team made every attempt to reach them personally so they would know what had happened before they returned. They also would know why productivity had slipped during that week. They would thus be prepared in advance to deal with that, as well as to anticipate their own lowered productivity once they returned.

In a location apart from the off-site space used for counseling, the team set up a command center. The new site was a visible means of demonstrating support for employees and the crisis team. For employees, the site served as a central meeting place where they could talk with and support each other during this time of crisis. In addition, the site allowed the crisis team members to remain physically separated from the media and other distractions, including the ongoing business. The team members wanted to focus on the crisis at hand.

The crisis team also made arrangements to inform employees in all the other locations what had happened, and the actions the company was taking to help the victims' families and the surviving employees.

Involving Employees in the Recovery Process

One of the decisions the crisis team made after their initial planning was to engage Wakefield employees as much as possible in the recovery. McComber said, "We involved our employees in many of the decisions we made during the next week, including when to return to work, how to acknowledge the lives of those murdered, and how to handle the affected worksite."

Employees gladly stepped up to the challenge. According to McComber, "They were very considerate and thoughtful in their comments and ideas. Staff members made some important suggestions, such as using members of middle management to work the hotline, making one-on-one counseling available 24 hours a day, holding a company-sponsored memorial service for the victims, and delaying the formal return to work until one week after the shooting."

Coming Back to Work

Employees returned to work one week after the shooting. It was a week of adjustment, and the Wakefield site leaders allowed people to select the number of hours they wished to work. "There wasn't much being accomplished, but it gave staff the opportunity to come together at the Wakefield location," McComber said. "Most took time off to attend all the memorial services and visit the homes of the victims. We allowed those who did not wish to return to the Wakefield location to work at the command center as long as they wanted to."

The crisis team scheduled the memorial service for the victims a few days after the formal return to work, in early January 2001. Volunteers spoke about each person, sharing details of their working life together at Edgewater. "It was extremely touching and was a way for them to express their love and appreciation to each one," McComber remembered.

External Communications

Company representatives addressed the media only through the communications specialists, who also produced all press releases. By consolidating communications through one source, the company was able to limit mistakes or misunderstandings that might have occurred if several people had given interviews or statements. This process also allowed leaders to focus more of their energy on employees. The company did hold a press conference the Friday after the Tuesday shooting to communicate how employees were coping and what the company was doing for them and for the victims' families.

Follow-up

Edgewater Technology set up a foundation for the victims' families and made a donation. They also encouraged donations from employees and the community. According to McComber, this was another way to show support for the families. It was also a way for employees at other Edgewater Technology sites to do something constructive.

Even though people returned to work shortly after the incident, its aftereffects continue five years later. The employee gunman went to trial in 2002. As of December 2005, he is in jail after being convicted of seven counts of first-degree murder. His appeal is pending.

Lessons in Leading

Five years later, McComber reflected on her own reactions to the situation: "It was an emotional two weeks for me. I felt I was on autopilot most of the time, but it was necessary for me to remain strong while giving our staff and others the support they needed. I started out functioning purely on gut instinct and ended up leading the efforts on all the people issues faced by the team." The CEO was responsible for the corporate focus and the face presented to the press. HR and the corporate counsel, as well as outside counsel, dealt with the legal implications of the tragedy.

McComber continued, "Only after I returned to my home in Little Rock did I begin to let myself grieve for those who had died and for their families. I felt we had done our very best and had given everyone the greatest possible support during the crisis. It was a daunting time, but we came through it, and the organization slowly returned to being productive. So did I."

With the benefit of hindsight, McComber noted that it would have been helpful to train employees and managers to recognize signs in employees who might be suffering from abuse, suppressed rage, or any number of other emotional conditions.

Nonetheless, the feedback from employees was very positive concerning the actions the Edgewater Technology leaders took during and after the shootings. "The majority felt we had provided them the support and counseling they needed," McComber said.

Tips for Managing the Human Element

The keys to managing the human side of of a crisis such as the one that befell Edgewater Technology include:

- Putting employees first and getting help to them, as well as to the victims' families, immediately

- Pulling together a senior management team and having them meet daily to work through all of the issues
- Recruiting experts to help the senior management team and the employees, especially for behavioral health issues and sensitive media issues
- Involving employees in as many decisions as possible (for a natural disaster, this may occur after you've started the business recovery)
- Communicating regularly both to inform and to alleviate anxieties

These actions are time-intensive and energy draining. Yet they can produce a multitude of benefits as employees recognize that you're just not saying you care for them, but you're also showing them you do. You're a true leader and employer of choice.

Muster Sites

"Muster sites" are a valuable part of a company's disaster toolkit that more employers should be using, according to crisis management expert Gerard Braud of Gerard Braud Communications, based in the New Orleans area. Braud describes muster sites as either physical or virtual sites where employees can gather to find one another, exchange information, and enlist support.

For example, using such a site the Edgewater Technology employees at Wakefield could gather at the command center to talk, grieve, share experiences, and start to recover and think about returning to work.

Braud believes that special websites for companies and communities play an important role in disseminating updates, gathering useful information, and encouraging a sense of belonging. If individuals know to visit a website after a disaster, they can get up-to-the minute information. Plus they can voluntarily provide their own contact information, such as the temporary address where they're staying, the phone number, and other pertinent facts. Some towns and businesses adversely affected by Hurricane Katrina were able to do this, and it helped people find one another and built a greater sense of community during a tumultuous experience.

Action Steps

1. Consider the special steps taken by Edgewater mangement in incorporating employee care into your business continuity planning.
2. Use the Wakefield example as a tabletop scenario to practice managing this type of crisis.
3. Think about how you can use "muster sites" to enhance employee communications during a disaster.

Appendix

Managing Stress after a Disaster
A Guide for Employees

This is an example of the material that First Interstate provided employees after the building fire described in the Prologue. Mory Framer, the trauma expert, developed it and has given his permission to include it here. This guide should be customized to your organization's situation, including its ability to provide for outside help.

We hope you will never have to refer to this handout. But if you are ever a victim of a disaster, you can expect to experience after-effects to varying degrees, and they can last anywhere from six weeks to three months or more.

We also want to alert you that there can be a ripple effect through your family and other loved ones. This handout is designed to help you through the healing process. The acknowledgement of emotional reactions helps shorten recovery time and prevent complications. Reactions can vary widely from one day to the next. *Don't be alarmed by the reemergence of emotions after days or weeks.*

Some Reactions You May Experience

- A sense that your life is out of balance
- Disbelief
- Repeated flashbacks
- Excessive sadness
- Repeated nightmares and other sleep disturbances
- Withdrawal from usually pleasurable activities
- Diminished sexual drive
- Frequent anger and irritability
- Forgetfulness and impaired concentration
- A sense of guilt at surviving

Self-Help Techniques

Don't push thoughts and memories of the event away; talk about them. Don't feel embarrassed about a repetitious need to talk to people.

Keep your life in balance by:

- Maintaining a healthful diet and getting adequate sleep and exercise
- Balancing your work with recreation and rest
- Avoiding new major projects in life
- Keeping a routine with family, close friends, and familiar surroundings

Seeking Help

Do not hesitate to contact behavioral health consultants or the Employee Assistance Program when any of the following occur:

- You or your family have questions regarding what you are feeling.
- You notice any significant changes in family patterns.
- You are suddenly experiencing new physical aches or pains or the aggravation of a physical illnesses. (You might be expressing emotional discomfort through your body.)
- Your normal sleep is significantly disrupted.
- You are bothered by persistent sadness, irritability, or nervousness.
- Your use of alcohol or sleep aids increases.
- A gradual reduction in symptoms does not occur.

Chapter 5

Guiding Managers and HR Staff

This chapter covers the following topics:
- How First Interstate's Human Resources team developed specialized training programs for HR staff, line managers, workers' compensation/risk insurance staff, and internal employee assistance counselors to increase awareness of the behavioral issues that could arise from the trauma of the building fire
- The definition of roles and responsibilities in a new coaching and counseling system that balanced the special needs of employees with the need to protect the company from needless workers' compensation claims and other liabilities
- How communications partners with HR

Overview

After the First Interstate fire, we had to relocate all employees quickly to new work sites. As we HR leaders dealt with employees' confusion, frustration, fear, and anger, we realized that we needed to take some direct and positive actions. We had to smooth the way for employees at all levels to learn how to deal with the situation directly, especially the trauma they were experiencing, so they could get back to work.

As we debriefed the events as a group, we realized we had to avoid getting caught up in what some people refer to as hindsight bias—how we thought we should have acted, once we knew what had actually happened with the fire, the recovery, and the restoration. After all, the fire required us to act quickly in a dynamic situation. Disasters by their very nature require you to dive into the unknown and take action. We had our priorities straight: ensuring that everyone was safe. And we fought rather than fled, which was the right thing to do.

Enlisting Expertise

We acknowledged that we needed professional help to equip ourselves, our managers, and our employees to deal effectively with the trauma caused by the fire. So we brought in Dr. Mory Framer, a specialist in trauma response and recovery. He had been instrumental in counseling a large contingent of search-and-rescue workers who had been assigned to grisly airplane and ferry crashes.

Dr. Framer's advice was twofold: first, take care of your employees; and second, take care of your organization. By taking care of the organization, leaders could ameliorate potential workers' compensation claims and other costs.

As a result of all the disasters we faced, First Interstate discovered other business benefits to taking care of employees first and the business second. These include employees returning to work so that the business can operate, preserving or even improving the company's reputation, and generating good will among employees and customers, which can help the company's bottom line over time. Other companies have also experienced these benefits.

Developing Special Employee Relations Training Programs

Dr. Framer designed and developed targeted training programs for employees in several departments: HR employee relationship managers, line managers, the medical group, the workers' compensation staff, and the Employee Assistance Program, which was an internal group. We also restated the responsibilities of these groups so we would all be clear on who would be doing what for the near term. Those statements are included at the end of this chapter.

Following is a synopsis of the training, with some suggestions on additional issues you may wish to consider.

Human Resources

HR staff received training in several techniques. Although HR professionals know how to mediate employee relations issues, they may not always know how to confront the behavioral underpinnings of stress, abject fear, anger, ennui, depression, or any of the stages of the grieving process—all of which disasters can trigger. We learned to intervene early so that we could help supervisors and employees come to grips with personal or interpersonal issues that either stemmed from the fire or were exacerbated by it.

We also worked on our skills for evaluating why the performance of some employees began to deteriorate after the incident. We took into consideration the pressures caused by the fire—dislocation from one's work space and other inconveniences that the employee may have been experiencing that could be contributing to a decline in performance. For example, had the employee been in a fire before? We received additional training on how and when to refer employees to the EAP.

Managers and Supervisors

Managerial and supervisory personnel received special training on how to reduce stress and tension at their work sites. They were encouraged to spend lots of face time with their employees by holding frequent all-hands meetings as well as one-on-one sessions. Managers and supervisors learned the importance of asking their employees about their situations, including how they were coping and how they felt about their working conditions, workloads, and other aspects of their jobs.

Managers and supervisors were also urged to give their staff members "mental health days" that would not count against their vacation or sick days. We also persuaded them to schedule departmental potlucks, picnics, ice cream breaks, pizza parties, and other gatherings to break the tension and have a bit of fun. For example, one department made a practice of taking lunch breaks out of the office, riding a downtown shuttle together for a change of scenery and different types of food.

Back then, managers and their employees often worked side by side. These days, a manager is often responsible for employees in multiple locations spread all over the world. That poses its own set of challenges when a disaster strikes. Nonetheless, one of the lessons we learned is that people want and need to spend time together. So if you're a manager who's not physically with your people, try to travel and be with them as much as possible. And for the times when you can't make it, ask people in the remote locale to gather together. Just make sure they don't spend all their time together wallowing in the hardship that befell them. It's fine to spend a little time in "pity city," but you must then switch the conversation to other issues, including planning for the future.

The managerial training also addressed employee performance issues. Managers learned to take additional time to examine why an employee's performance was declining. We discouraged them from jumping immediately into the disciplinary process. We also had them learn more about the Employee Assistance Program and the importance of referring a troubled employee to a counselor immediately following the detection of a behavioral or stress-induced problem.

Chapter 6 includes instructions for dealing with specific behavioral conditions caused by trauma. These instructions will work in any trauma situation. At the bank, we put great emphasis on reporting, not because we were the ultimate "personnel police," but because we needed the paper trail for business protection purposes.

Employee Assistance

Employee assistance staff received supplementary training to identify signs and symptoms of delayed or post-traumatic stress syndrome. They learned applicable therapeutic techniques and how to identify the most appropriate sources of outside support and expertise for extreme cases.

For example, about two weeks after the fire, HR staff learned that two employees had been working on the 16th floor late the night the fire broke out below them, on the 12th floor. They smelled and saw smoke and assumed it was related to the welding project that was under way to retrofit the sprinkler system. (To our horror, we also learned belatedly that the sprinkler system had been shut off at night while this retrofitting was occurring.)

As the smoke thickened and turned black, the two employees realized something dreadful was happening. They hopped in an elevator, which—amazingly—took them through the fire to the lobby. They then ran outside through the thick, dark, suffocating smoke to the street. It was only then that they saw flames shooting out of the building, felt hot glass shards hitting them, and discovered they were in the midst of a fire.

Their trauma started soon after. When we learned of their plight two weeks later, we arranged for comprehensive psychological counseling with extensive follow-up. They slowly recovered and overcame their nightmares, and were able to return to a productive level of work.

But their fear and trauma came rushing back when they were assigned to the 37th floor of the building, in the exact place where two other employees had been trapped and then rescued. Scratch marks were visible all over the windows where they had tried unsuccessfully to break the glass.

With one phone call, the trauma counselor came back on site *immediately* to help them along with all the other employees on that floor. The counselor helped them learn to deal with the daily reminders of not just one but two frightening experiences.

Workers' Compensation Department

Staff responsible for workers' compensation benefits were taught to identify any claims related to the fire and to perform case interviews as soon as possible. As a result of the training we conducted for all our special groups after the fire, only two claims were submitted. These were filed by the two people who were caught in the burning building and suffered smoke inhalation. There were no claims for stress or any other fire-related conditions.

With just two workers' compensation claims and no litigation, our investment in this training more than paid for itself.

HR Partnership with the EAP

Although HR had worked well with the Employee Assistance Program staff before the fire, we became even more aware of the pivotal role EAP played in the care of our people, so the relationship became much closer. We maintained our commitment to the confidential nature of the EAP and made sure no confidences were violated. In addition, the HR staff gained a stronger understanding of the power of healing through the types of interventions the EAP could make.

Today most organizations outsource medical and EAP services, and encourage employees to take more responsibility for managing their careers and their personal lives. Nonetheless, employers can still make available off-the-shelf programs in such areas as stress management, relaxation techniques, nutrition, and exercise. First Interstate was large enough and fortunate enough to have a corporate industrial nurse on staff. The nurse, along with the EAP, helped us conduct group programs based on Dr. Framer's principles that were necessary to take care of our people. Employees understood the value of these programs, especially in the wake of a disaster, and attended them in high numbers.

Responsibility Structure

In addition to developing department-specific training programs, we devised a responsibility structure enabling all affected managers, HR leaders, and individuals in other key functions noted to remain clear on who was responsible for what once it was established that employees were safe and we were ready to return to work. A disaster is no time for silo thinking or operating. Leaders need to work together across functional lines to take care of managers, employees, and the organization.

Although each situation is different, you should address this role clarification as you build your business continuity plan. We had to devise our structural outline during the emergency; we can only imagine how much more effective we could have been if this had been in place as part of the business continuity plan.

By the time our next disaster struck, we were much better prepared to help HR staff and managers deal with the trauma, and our managers and employees both noticed and appreciated this.

Managers/Supervisors

Role: To closely monitor performance levels of all employees and refer to support professionals to facilitate early problem solving.

Responsibilities:

- Monitor performance of employees.
- Intervene quickly to identify issues if performance begins to decline.

- Refer employees to support professionals.
- Advise HR representative about employee relations issue.
- Document performance decline in regular reports, with a copy to HR.
- Be sensitive to needs and problems of employees.
- Be aware of trends or problems developing in the department.

Human Resources Managers

Role: To assist managers with early problem detection, evaluate employee issues, and refer employees to support professionals.

Responsibilities:

- Sensitize managers to employee relations issues.
- Educate managers and supervisors in the early detection of problems and the importance of documentation and follow-through.
- Provide counsel to managers in evaluating employee relations issues.
- Attend intervention meeting as requested by managers/supervisors or employees.
- Refer employee to the Employee Assistance counselor or the corporate nurse as necessary.
- Follow up with managers/supervisors or employees to confirm that meetings with the Employee Assistance counselor or the corporate nurse have taken place.
- Intervene with managers or supervisors experiencing difficulties.
- Schedule debriefing/tension reduction meetings to identify and follow up on issues.
- Be sensitive to trends or problems developing in departments or groups.
- Review reports received from managers/supervisors and follow up as necessary.
- Complete summaries for senior HR management as requested.
- Provide recommendations to senior HR management and Employee Assistance staff regarding departmental issues or concerns.

Employee Assistance Counselors

Employee Assistance counselors included staff members and independent contractors who were brought in to assist staff because of the large number of cases.

Role: To provide professional counseling for employees who need assistance with personal problems, stress management, and other issues and refer employees as necessary for outside assistance.

Responsibilities:

- Counsel employees who have requested counseling or have been referred by a manager or HR representative.
- Refer employees who may need assistance from outside professionals.
- Advise the HR representative of any problems or trends developing in a department.
- Advise the HR representative about coordinating assistance for departments requiring debriefing or tension reduction sessions.
- Conduct and/or attend debriefing or tension reduction sessions, whenever possible.
- Advise senior HR managers regarding overall company trends or problems.
- Educate managers/supervisors and HR staff in early problem detection and intervention techniques.

Corporate Nurse

Role: To provide assistance and/or referrals to employees who have general health complaints.

Responsibilities:

- Provide medical attention to referred employees experiencing health problems.
- Refer employees who need counseling to Employee Assistance counselors.
- Advise HR representatives and/or EAP counselors about any problems or trends developing in a department.
- Offer assistance to departments or individuals as necessary, including techniques for stress reduction and self-help.

Corporate Communications

Communications also plays a critical role. This may or may not be part of the HR function, but a strong partnership between the two is vital in any type of crisis. Here are examples of communications roles and responsibilities, which can be handled most effectively by partnering with HR.

Role: To communicate with employees, media, and other key audiences as quickly, accurately, comprehensively, and consistently as possible and to encourage two-way communications.

Responsibilities:

- Provide counsel to leaders and HR on internal and external communications issues, especially those related to the safety of employees and the reputation of the company.

- Be prepared to adjust plans and actions as the situation warrants, including changing the "voice" of the company.

- Be in frequent contact with the local media, especially local radio and TV newscasters whose stations have their own news-gathering departments.

- Keep up-to-date fact sheets about the organization, including stock photos and videos.

- Partner with HR and IT to develop telephone trees that include home telephone as well as cell phone numbers and personal e-mail addresses so that you can notify employees quickly and continue to communicate with them.

- Work with IT to create alternative websites and set up toll-free phone numbers that employees can refer to after a disaster strikes; consider a separate number and site for customers and media.

- Coordinate with safety/security to allow for the inclusion of communications, especially employee communications, in their plans, procedures, and policies.

- Ensure that communications staff have the necessary supplies to communicate under all circumstances, especially in the event of a power outage or the loss of the entire telecommunications structure (e.g., satellite phones, battery-operated radios and TVs, power chargers that will work with a car battery, hand-cranked or battery-operated chargers for cell phones and PDAs, paper, pens and pencils, etc.).

- Clarify roles among the communications staff, especially in terms of internal and external communications and shifts of operations.
- Make arrangements for backup support, including such resources as communications staff in other offices around the globe or an outside agency in another city.
- Be ready to intervene if managers/supervisors or others in the organization are found to be experiencing difficulties or disseminating misinformation.
- Schedule debriefing meetings with HR, the EAP, Safety/Security, and managers to assess how well messages are getting through, what else needs to be communicated, and what other communications actions are needed.
- Regularly remind employees of the actions they need to take, both at work and at home, if a disaster strikes.

Action Steps

1. Consider how you will deal with the behavioral issues that can result from a disaster. There are examples and lessons throughout the book that you can draw on. See especially Chapters 7 and 8.
2. Define roles and responsibilities among the following groups for dealing with these issues and determine how they will partner during an emergency:
   a. Human Resources staff
   b. Line managers
   c. Workers' compensation/risk management staff
   d. Communications staff
3. Read Chapter 6 on the results of First Interstate Bank's efforts toward balancing the needs of employees with the need to get back to work.

Chapter 6

Balancing the Needs of Employees with the Need to Return to Work

This chapter discusses the following topics:
- Helping employees through the trauma caused by a disaster
- The signs of disaster-related performance problems
- Guidelines for a meeting with an employee who is having trouble
- Tips for interviewing a troubled employee

Getting Back to Work after a Disaster

Once the rains, winds, fire, or floodwaters have abated, it's time to attend in equal parts to employees' physical and emotional states in anticipation of going back to work. You need to consider where your employees will report to work; whether they have the tools, information, and other resources they need to do their jobs; and what tasks they need to focus on. As daunting as this may seem considering everything that has happened, the challenges of getting employees established in a new work setting may be nothing compared with dealing with their emotional states.

As a leader, you may have to deal with employees' feelings of loss, uncertainty, confusion, fear, sadness, anxiety, and anger. You may need to deal with issues of safety, health, and job security.

When you and your employees are forced to work under difficult conditions, frustrations—both theirs and yours—can work against the organization's objectives.

Getting Business Systems Up and Running

In the hours and days after a disaster strikes, organization leaders frequently become consumed with the logistics of business interruption. In fact, most business continuity plans concentrate on backup computer facilities, backup mechanical systems, off-site locations for resuming work, and perhaps an Emergency Operations Center that has sufficient space for the executives most critical to command and control efforts.

Balancing Employee Needs with the Business

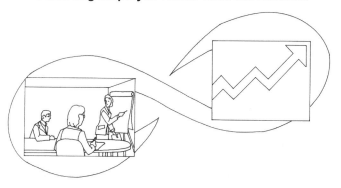

Returning People to Productivity

But what about backup human systems? What planning have you devoted to employees whose homes have been destroyed? What are you doing to help those who can't get to the work site or those who can't get home from work? What about those with missing family members or those who are separated from their family and pets?

As explained in Chapter 2, you need to build these considerations into your business continuity plan, and develop appropriate contingent Human Resources policies. As a rule of thumb, acts of nature that cut a wide or deep swath across society can have effects more devastating and longer-lasting than a company-specific problem, such as a plant explosion or a building fire. That's why it's so important to think broadly when preparing for disasters. If you are to resume your business operations, you need employees back at work.

Northeastern Ohio is several hundred miles from tornado alley. But that didn't stop a twister one Friday evening in 1985 from bisecting the Delphi auto parts plant there, where Michael Hissam, now the Regional Director of Corporate Affairs for Delphi's Mexico operations, worked as lead media contact. The plant, which ran multiple shifts, had a disaster preparedness plan, which was immediately put into action. Even though the plan hadn't taken tornados into account, it was comprehensive enough that the plant was able to resume operations the first thing Monday morning.

Not all employees went back to work. One employee lost her life at the plant, and more than 200 had been injured either there or in the neighboring area. Others lost their homes. Hissam recalls that it took months for some people to recover, not only from their physical injuries but also from their property damage and the trauma. Other employees pitched in to cover for their absentee co-workers, and many contributed money to help ease the financial strain. Members of the HR staff spent time helping affected employees and their families.

In early January 2005, 30 inches of rain fell in Santa Barbara, California, over a two-week period Normal rainfall is less than half that amount. The typically dry, rocky riverbeds were now whitewater torrents rushing to the sea and in some cases overflowing their banks. An area south of Santa Barbara suffered a horrendous landslide; 10 people were killed and the only north-south highway was closed to traffic in both directions for more than a week. As if that weren't enough, at the north end of the Santa Barbara coastline, another stretch of the same highway was closed for a day because of an overturned truck as well as mudslides and overflowing creeks.

Thus, the area was landlocked, and employers were faced with the dilemma of how to keep their operations going with some employees stuck at work and others stuck at home. Managers scrambled to find hotel rooms for those employees at work. Some of the employees who were stranded at home could work from there. But many people were not working, or were working shortened schedules and having difficulty concentrating when they were working. Employees were concerned about access to adequate food, shelter, and clothing, not to mention their paychecks.

Employers asked themselves, "Do we pay or not pay?" Some employers could pay and did so. Others decided they could not afford to pay for time not worked, but did allow their non-exempt employees to use vacation pay. This underscores the importance of developing contingent pay policies based on your financial capabilities. Some employers, after Katrina or a similar disaster, were able to reassure their employees with full pay for a limited period of time. Pay or no pay, some employees may decide to move on, and this can really throw a wrench into a company's business recovery process. "Employees and management are not drinking the same Kool-Aid®," observes Charles Pizzo, crisis communication expert and Hurricane Katrina evacuee. Employees have a lot more on their minds than returning to work. "Employees' first responsibility is to themselves and their families. They're concerned about their self-preservation; they're thinking about their safety, not their work." This is especially true of employees in a minimum-wage job.

An employer that fails to create a sound plan for dealing with disasters and getting the business back on track while attending to the employees' needs, Pizzo says, runs a big risk of losing employees. "By not taking actions, either to plan or to take actions afterward to help, employers (particularly those in the service industry with lots of low-level customer-facing jobs) are leaving their businesses totally vulnerable."

Employee Trauma

Getting employees back to work after a crisis is just the first step. Trauma experts and others who are familiar with the human systems side of business continuity planning know that crises can contribute to tension in the workplace, which manifests itself in various ways. In addition to a high attrition rate, a business can suffer costly workers' compensation claims, spiraling medical costs, excessive absenteeism, and loss of productivity. And these problems may continue long after the emergency has passed.

The managers and supervisors who are most familiar with the work habits and personalities of their employees can play a critical role in preventing problems, detecting difficulties, and motivating people to accept outside help. HR can help by recommending outside resources, the costs of which may be covered by the company.

Everyone needs to look out for everyone else. The detection and solution of problems early in the post-catastrophe period can bring benefits to employees and the company alike. Employees will experience less trauma, or can at least recover and grow stronger more quickly. Co-workers who aren't suffering the adverse affects of the disaster won't feel as burdened or resentful because of the extra work they've taken on. As a result, morale can improve faster, and employee relations will be better.

By dealing promptly and directly with employee trauma, an employer can minimize its exposure to costly workers' compensation claims as well as medical and disability claims. Employers also may increase attendance and reduce tardiness faster than they would otherwise, which will increase their chances of maintaining satisfactory productivity levels.

Everyone, especially managers and those in HR, should remain extra sensitive to the needs and problems of employees. Managers should be aware of unusual behavioral trends or problems developing in their departments. Be sure to consider each employee as an individual, because everyone can react differently. A manager or HR staff member who spots an employee problem should immediately refer the person to a trained professional who can help identify the nature of the problem and then work to solve it. This professional can be a resource in HR or an Employee Assistance Program (EAP) resource. Chapter 8 gives detailed information on the value of specialized EAP trauma counseling.

If you're a manager, you need to work with the Human Resources staff and the EAP counselor (if you have elected to use this service) to determine if it would be best to put the employee on a short (e.g., one month) leave of absence to give the individual time for counseling and recovery. If so, then upon the employee's return, you will need to sit down together and establish performance expectations that are reasonable and fair both to the employee and to the employer.

Responses to Performance Decline

Managers and supervisors must take specific steps if an employee's performance begins to decline:

1. Intervene quickly, referring the employee to support professionals such as HR staff, the EAP, and/or other available behavioral health professionals.

2. Refer the employee to a professional at every step in the problem-solving or disciplinary process, including verbal warning, written warning, and probation, and document these offers of assistance.

This is different from the normal progressive disciplinary process in that you are offering *behavioral health assistance* along the way.

3. Follow up to ensure that the employee has met with support professionals.
4. Make sure you or HR staff members are advised about employee relations issues.
5. Make sure that managers document signs of performance decline and referrals they have made and that they send a copy to HR.

Documentation is essential to support the problem-solving process and in responding to litigation or workers' compensation claims. The information must be accurate, factual, and consistent. Record specific behavior: "Employee missed meeting on 6/15/06 without giving a reason." "I detected alcohol on employee's breath 7/23/06." "Employee arrived 40 minutes late for work on 8/20/06 with no explanation." Also include information about referrals: "I recommended getting counseling through the EAP." You can find a sample documentation form on page 101 at the end of this chapter.

When documenting behavior, don't include hearsay and don't judge or diagnose the cause of an employee's actions. Contact the behavioral health resource with your performance documentation. Although this approach is always important, it becomes essential if the employee denies having a problem. Refer to the "dos and don'ts" at the end of this chapter before completing the documentation.

Specific Performance Problems

The following behavioral problems are warning signals that managers need to recognize and document:

1. Absenteeism, including:
   a. Unauthorized leave
   b. Excessive sick leave
   c. Monday absences, Friday absences, or Monday *and* Friday absences (could be related to increased alcohol or drug usage)
   d. Repeated absences of two to four days
   e. More than one absence of one to two weeks (5 to 10 days)
   f. Excessive tardiness, especially on Monday mornings or when returning from lunch (again, may be a sign of substance abuse)
   g. Often leaving work early

h. Peculiar and increasingly implausible excuses for absences
i. Higher absenteeism rate relative to other employees for colds, flu, gastritis, and common ailments (and, consequently, more claims on health insurance)
2. "On-the-job absenteeism," for example:
   a. Continual absence from workstation beyond what the job requires
   b. Frequent trips to water fountain or bathroom
   c. Long coffee breaks
   d. Physical illness on the job
3. High accident rate, including:
   a. Accidents on the job
   b. Frequent trips to nurse's office
   c. Accidents off the job but affecting job performance
4. Difficulty concentrating, for example:
   a. Greater effort required
   b. Longer time spent per job
   c. Hand tremor during concentration
5. Confusion, for example:
   a. Difficulty recalling instructions and details of work assignments
   b. Increasing difficulty in dealing with complex assignments
   c. Problems recalling one's own mistakes
6. Spasmodic work patterns—for instance, alternating periods of very high and low productivity
7. Inflexibility—does not change easily. Your requests for change may present a threat because the employee's control over present job duties and responsibilities allows him or her to hide low job performance. The inability to make routine changes could also indicate a high tension level or another serious problem.
8. Coming or returning to work in an atypical condition, which may indicate a substance abuse problem
9. Generally lowered job efficiency, for example:
   a. Missed deadlines
   b. Mistakes due to inattention or poor judgment
   c. More material wasted
   d. Bad decisions
   e. Complaints from customers
   f. Implausible excuses for poor job performance

10. Poor personal relationships on the job
11. Friction with other employees, usually resulting in decreased job performance and efficiency
12. Possible alcoholism or drug addiction, as suggested by the following behavior:
    a. Overreacts to real or imagined criticism
    b. Exhibits wide mood swings
    c. Borrows money from co-workers
    d. Compiles complaints from co-workers
    e. Harbors unreasonable resentments
    f. Begins to avoid associates

Meeting with an Employee Who Is Having Trouble

Meeting with an employee face to face to discuss a problem is never an easy task. You may be tempted to put off a confrontation with someone who is troubled. Or you may meet with the person but hesitate to recommend counseling. You must overcome your reluctance, however, because an employee who is in trouble usually knows it and is often relieved to have the problem out in the open so it can be dealt with.

You can simplify the confrontation with an employee having job performance problems by breaking it down as follows:

1. If you notice any of the preceding behaviors, or your employee's performance is clearly declining, intervene quickly to determine the key issue(s) that are responsible.

2. Meet with your employee at his or her workstation or office if the level of privacy is adequate. Come prepared with a clear definition of the job criteria and the facts that you wish to address; for example, in the case of excessive absenteeism, have the problem dates in front of you. You might begin by saying, "I've been concerned about you lately. I've noticed you missed work on June 10, 11, and 18, and you're missing department deadlines; you just haven't been your usual self."

3. Focus on specific job performance issues or behaviors, not on vague personality or attitude problems, which can easily be denied. Indicate the effect that the worker's problem is having on you, on the workload, and on the other workers in your unit.

4. Hold an unhurried discussion and maintain sensitivity to the employee's feelings and needs. The manner in which you address your employee in this first meeting will be critical in reducing his or her defensiveness and creating a comfortable environment for communication.

5. Listen carefully to the employee. Be empathetic. Avoid minimizing what he or she is feeling or saying. Maintain a calm, supportive, and positive tone. Continue to gently ask questions and listen until you fully understand the nature of the problem, including its relationship to the recent disaster.

6. Be careful not to over-emotionalize what is said. Communicate the facts and discuss the issues.

7. Continue to be supportive but firm in the message that his or her performance must return to a satisfactory level. Remain calm and firm, always bringing the conversation back to specific on-the-job problems, despite any excuses, defensiveness, or hostility on the part of your employee.

8. Avoid any diagnosis or labeling of the employee's problem. Stress that whatever the trouble is, it is the employee's responsibility to do whatever is necessary—for instance, meet with an Employee Assistance counselor or a behavioral health provider—for him or her to perform adequately. If necessary, offer to schedule an appointment for the employee yourself.

9. If the problem involves personal matters—for example, family troubles, alcohol or drug abuse, stress, or financial worries—either directly or indirectly brought on by the disaster, be particularly sensitive and respectful of the employee's feelings. It is difficult for anyone except a professional counselor to assist in these situations. Reassure your employee that the company wants to help through the EAP or other resource.

10. Keep an open door and follow up to ensure that the employee meets with a trained counselor, such as one provided by the EAP.

11. Emphasize exactly what you expect the employee to do to resolve the problem. Be sure that the employee understands, and then get a commitment and monitor progress.

12. Set a definite date—a month later, perhaps—for your next meeting, at which time you expect to see marked improvement.

13. End the interview on a positive note, voicing your expectation that, given the resources available, the employee will start to deal with the problem and his or her work productivity will improve.

If you have asked your employee to make an appointment with the Employee Assistance Program or a behavioral health provider, contact the provider to advise them that you have referred this person. Confidentiality will always be maintained between the provider and the employee, but the provider can tell you when your employee has met with them and if he or she is cooperating.

Dos and Don'ts for the Employee Meeting

Do:

- Focus solely on the declining job performance and your offer to help.
- Have written documentation for the declining job performance on hand so that you can let the record speak for itself.
- Maintain a firm and formal yet considerate attitude. If the interview becomes a casual or intimate conversation, the impact of the message will be lessened.
- Explain that help is available through the EAP, and emphasize that all aspects of the program are completely confidential.
- State that the employee's decision about his or her preference to seek or not to seek professional help will be considered in reevaluating his or her performance at a later date.

Don't:

- Try to find out what is wrong with the employee.
- Allow yourself to get involved in the employee's personal life.
- Make generalizations or insinuations about the employee's performance.
- Moralize; restrict your criticism to job performance.
- Be misled by sympathy-evoking tactics. Stay focused on your right to expect appropriate behavior and satisfactory job performance.
- Threaten discipline unless you are willing and able to carry out the threat.

First Corrective Interview

If the employee's performance continues to deteriorate, conduct another interview and take whatever means of disciplinary action is warranted. Inform the employee that failure to improve job performance will result in further disciplinary action up to and including termination. Conclude with a strong recommendation that the individual use the services of the Employee Assistance Program.

Second Corrective Interview

If the employee's performance continues to deteriorate, conduct a second corrective interview. Conclude by offering the employee the choice between accepting the services of the Employee Assistance Program or being terminated because of unsatisfactory job performance.

Termination

If, after the steps described above, the employee does not or will not perform to the position's job performance standards, he or she should be terminated.

Remember, the goal is to balance business continuity with the needs of *all* employees. If employees in a given work group can't count on a co-worker to perform, this hurts everyone's performance and creates even more tension when nerves may still be raw from the disaster.

Action Steps

1. Design your own approach to training managers in advance on:
   a. Dealing with traumatized employees
   b. Recognizing the symptoms
   c. Referring employee for help or putting employee on leave
   d. Conducting special performance interviews
   e. Providing warnings
   f. Terminating employees

2. Consider developing a brief manager's guide for dealing with traumatized employees that managers can keep with the other business continuity planning materials that you will provide.
3. Plan for a quick refresher course with managers if you do experience a disaster.

Employee Counseling Report

Employee name ID number				Date	
Department name			Job title		Grade/Level
Hire date	Mail stop	Employee phone	Supervisor's name and title		
Relocated from (X site)			Current location		

Please describe the employee's issues, or the performance problem as you see it.

When did your first notice this problem?

Has the employee made you aware of any extenuating circumstances outside the workplace that could be affecting performance? Yes _____ No _____. If yes, please list:

Did employee initiate contact with the supervisor or HR staff member? Yes _____ No_____
If so, when (date)? _____

Has employee been referred to EAP provider for counseling? Yes _____ No _____
If so, when (date)? _____ By whom?

Significant dates and events:

Date(s) _____ Event(s) _____
_____   _____
_____   _____

Other persons having knowledge of the problems:

Resolution requested by employee

Recommendations made to employee

Employee referred to: (if applicable)

Completed by (name and date):

Date of follow-up	Follow-up comments	Disposition

Final disposition:

Please forward a copy of this report to _____ as soon as possible.

Chapter 7

Restabilizing Yourself and the Organization

This chapter describes 10 actions you can take to help you get back on your feet and the organization back to profitability.

Overview

When the ground shifts—either literally or figuratively—you may find it difficult to regain your balance, much less move forward in a deliberate, planned manner. Yet getting back to business may be just what employees and the organization need. Business as somewhat usual can be a welcome distraction as well as serving as a rallying cause and source of hope for the future. There are also practical reasons—the company needs to make up for lost time in meeting customer needs and demands, keeping competitors at bay, and fulfilling shareholder expectations.

10 Action Steps

Following are 10 actions you can take—in any order—to accelerate the recovery process for you, employees, and the organization.

1. Recognize That There Is No Getting Back to Normal

Getting back to work and getting back to normal are two different things. You can do the former but not the latter. It's important to acknowledge this fact as soon as possible. Just as you cannot step in the same river twice, you cannot go back to the way things were before a disaster. Your life and the lives of others have been permanently altered.

Delete the phrase "getting back to normal" from your vocabulary, and encourage others to do so. Instead, talk about creating a new state of normalcy that recognizes and builds on the changed circumstances.

To help people move forward rather than remain stuck in the past, address the need to work on mission-critical tasks such as serving customers and helping fellow employees cope. Also, encourage people to get professional help as needed.

2. Make Life a Little Easier

Look for ways to provide employees and their families with support that fosters peace of mind. The littlest things can mean a great deal at times like this, especially if they relieve anxiety and help people get through trying times.

Examples include toll-free numbers that people can call to get updates and other information and to leave messages; special websites with messaging boards; new cell phones, laptops, and briefcases to replace those destroyed or left behind; whistles for people concerned about getting stuck in an elevator; prepaid calling cards; reissued ID cards; flashlights and other battery-operated equipment; water; and food, lots of food.

Having breakfasts, lunches, and frequent snack breaks with other employees can aid in the healing process. The togetherness provides solace and gives people the opportunity to share their tales as well as offer tips for coping.

Also consider arranging for exercise classes, yoga, chair massages, and group walks; this will encourage people to take care of themselves physically too.

3. Expect the Unexpected in the Healing Process

Keep in mind that the healing process is nonlinear, very personal, and extremely complex. Individuals take different amounts of time to heal, based on their personal situations and past experiences, including prior traumas that may be unrelated to the disaster that just happened. It's also fairly common for people to take three steps forward followed by two steps back.

Don't be surprised if, five or six months (or even several years) after a disaster, some employees suffer a relapse or become uncomfortable with certain routines—such as flying, staying in a hotel, riding an elevator, or driving a route associated with an evacuation. These activities and others may bring back painful memories.

Some employees may prefer to avoid situations that remind them of the unpleasant event; this is a natural reaction that can help them heal. In any case, make sure that you as well as other managers are sensitive to these issues, and work to accommodate the needs of employees and their families. The goal is to provide a supportive environment without sacrificing business requirements. This can be achieved with some creativity and flexibility.

Encourage affected individuals to get screening and then, if needed, counseling and other support. Help them develop effective coping strategies working with the EAP or other community resources. Also support their participation in follow-up counseling services, especially if they have experienced multiple trauma events. Be aware that some individuals may develop post-traumatic stress disorder, in which case they should receive professional help. (Chapter 8 covers this situation in more detail.)

4. Communicate Often, Even When There Isn't Much News

People seek answers during a time of crisis, and they want to get information straight from the source, not just from all-news radio, TV, blogs, newspapers, or the grapevine, so make every effort to communicate frequently through a variety of channels.

Also, strive for a balance between messages that are inspirational and those that are practical yet honest. You don't want to distort reality. But when people are feeling uncertain, anxious, and impatient, they don't need to feel hopeless at the same time. Look for encouraging signs and convey confidence about the future while showing your support for employees' current day-to-day needs. Confidence, as long as it is grounded in reality, can give people the courage to carry on today and maintain hope for the future.

5. Be Visible and Persuade All Company Leaders to Do the Same

When leaders are visible, they send three key signals that are critical to recovery:

- They are aware of the impact of the disaster on people as well as on the business.

- They are taking measures to restore the business and the confidence of customers, investors, suppliers, and employees.
- They consider disaster recovery and business continuity top priorities.

Being visible also sends the message that the leaders are approachable and thus understanding and compassionate about the difficult times their employees are experiencing. And as leaders meet with employees in the cafeteria, hallways, and meeting rooms, they're able to get firsthand information from employees about their experiences. By gathering unfiltered information, the leaders will gain a better sense and appreciation of what's happening on the front lines.

If possible, during such times leaders should increase their face-to-face time with employees exponentially, especially compared with the amount of time spent sending e-mail and voice-mail messages. Technology is a faster and more efficient way to communicate, but it doesn't relay the powerful motivating messages that the personal touch does. For leaders to be most effective after a disaster, employees need to see and hear them in action.

6. Find Symbolic Actions That Will Build Credibility as Well as Engage and Inspire Employees

By being the first to move back into the building after a disastrous fire, as explained in the Prologue, the most senior managers at First Interstate Bank made a solid statement about safety. After the *Des Moines Register* recovered from a flood, the newspaper's management made T-shirts that said, "We survived the flood of '93." The shirts and the newspaper's later book, *Iowa's Lost Summer*, became treasured souvenirs of a shared ordeal.

Once the shock of a disaster has worn off, find ways for employees to help others, which in turn will help them. One example is the foundation that Edgewater Technology established for the murder victims' families. Another example is the action that leaders at BancFirst took after the 1995 Oklahoma City bombing. They organized the collection of needed items, such as bottled water and gloves, for the rescue workers toiling at the nearby Murrah Federal Building.

Also, regularly thank and recognize people for their contributions.

7. Encourage People to Talk and Tell Their Stories

It is human nature for people to relate what happened to them during a disaster to anyone who will listen. It's also natural for others to ask about the incident. Edgewater Technology encouraged its employees to talk to one another after the murders at its Wakefield office, described in Chapter 4. Managers at the Oklahoma City BancFirst did the same thing and suspended any ideas of productivity for the days immediately after the disaster.

Fostering two-way employee communication is an effective tool in all types of traumatic situations. For example, when Texas Instruments' chairman died unexpectedly, other leaders encouraged employees at all levels around the world to remember their fallen leader by sharing personal stories. These emotional exchanges not only were cathartic on an individual level but also connected employees across cultures, countries, and job levels. This sharing helped everyone to deal with their grief.

Taking a hit on productivity by encouraging employees to share their stories in the immediate aftermath of a crisis can pay dividends later because talking is a healthy first step to recovery. Days, weeks, months, and even years after an event, some individuals continue to find solace in talking about what happened as well as what they're currently doing, thinking, and feeling. They may also believe that others will better understand them and their point of view if they provide some context—that is, a description of what happened to them. While others may prefer to move on and not dwell on the past, it's important that you not rush to silence those who are not ready to put the events behind them.

Also, think about including first-person accounts in your employee publications or on your intranet, even if this is not standard policy. Writing can be healing and other employees may take their peers' advice more seriously if it's in a printed record of some kind, especially if their author-colleagues share lessons learned. For example, Agilent Technologies assigned a communications staff member to work with several employees to record their stories of helping with the 9/11 rescue efforts.

8. Adjust Policies, Procedures, and Processes as Necessary

Be reasonable about keeping the business going, and consider adjusting the rules to help employees do their jobs and get on with their lives. For instance, years ago, before laptop computers were common, Liz (the co-author) worked for a consulting firm with an ironclad rule that employees could check out a company-issue laptop for no more than three days in a row. When Liz learned that she would have to live in a hotel room indefinitely while her apartment and the rest of the building were being cleaned of asbestos after an explosion—which meant not having access to her home PC—she asked the office manager for a special waiver. The office manager said no; rules are rules. However, the leaders changed the policy when a cost-benefit calculation indicated that they could recover the cost of a new laptop in about two weeks by allowing Liz to work evenings and weekends in her hotel room.

In addition, the company accounting department was allowing no deviance from the rule that employees must submit original receipts with expense reports. That was a problem because Liz's original receipts were covered with asbestos dust on her dining room table, and she wouldn't have access to them for months, if ever. Rather than argue with accounting, Liz asked the credit card company to send her duplicate bills. The call center agent was cooperative and sympathetic, especially when told that Liz was one of the people left homeless after a steam pipe explosion in New York City, which was a national news story.

BancFirst in Oklahoma City didn't stick hard and fast to company rules concerning time off for attending funerals. The leaders there believed it was especially important for employees in the mortgage department to pay respects to their colleagues at HUD who had died in the 1995 bombing.

Being flexible and relaxing policies, procedures, and processes can go a long way toward helping employees return to productive work.

9. Redefine Professionalism to Fit the Situation

Professionalism does not mean being stoic or acting like a robot. Leaders should be able to express their own pain, grief, and other feelings in the aftermath of a disaster, as long as they're not contributing to the confusion. The leader who is able to reveal the individual behind the title is seen as more authentic, especially when he or she admits to not knowing all the answers and allows his or her own vulnerability to show. Employees can better connect with such leaders, not just mentally but also emotionally, and will be reassured and inspired by them.

This expression of feelings—especially being empathetic—should not be seen as conflicting with the need to remain dispassionate, which was discussed in Chapter 1. Rather, it supports the goal of staying connected to those around you, and showing that you understand what's happening.

10. Take Care of Yourself

Leaders are expected and obligated to safeguard their employees and the organization. But to maintain momentum and provide quality care, you need to look after yourself as well; this includes acknowledging your feelings and dealing with your own emotional state. See the sidebar, "Managing Yourself," for some suggestions.

Planning the Restabilization

Practicing the actions recommended in this chapter can speed up the healing process, which in turn can improve everyone's work performance and productivity. However, just as you cannot predict an emergency or disaster, you cannot anticipate exactly how you, other leaders, or your employees will react and recover.

If you regularly plan and practice simulations, you can at least get some idea of how people will respond. Nonetheless, the past, whether real or simulated, is a limited indicator of future performance. You need to be prepared for wide variations along the human dimension as you build your business continuity plan. Knowing the range of potential reactions and how to respond appropriately will go a long way toward helping you restabilize yourself, your employees, and the organization.

Managing Yourself

Suggestions from Mitchell M. Marks

Mitch Marks specializes in advising executives on managing mergers, restructurings, and other transitions. Over the years, Dr. Marks has suggested that individuals at all levels of an organization take the following actions when dealing with a stressful situation.

- Make an effort to build some quiet time into your schedule. Also exercise, eat carefully, get plenty of rest and relaxation, and practice other forms of stress management. This is especially important if the incident you're dealing with is drawn out or extremely intense. You cannot function successfully on autopilot for long stretches without some refueling.
- Be aware of your own feelings—such as anger, fatigue, withdrawal, and pain.
- Accept that you cannot have all the answers and cannot keep everybody happy. Just concentrate on making sure that everyone is physically and psychologically safe and is taking constructive steps toward recovery.
- Talk things out; get support from friends, family members, and other professionals. Consult people who have undergone similar experiences. Talking will help you recognize that you are not alone—a realization that in itself is helpful.
- Do some reality testing. Ask a diverse group of people for their reactions and feedback.
- Keep track of yourself and your experiences; take notes on what is going well and what is troubling you. Maintaining a journal can be very cathartic.
- Recognize what you can and cannot control, and remind yourself of this as needed.
- Be tolerant of those around you; this is a trying time for all involved. And remember that people respond differently to a given event and heal on very different schedules.
- Be tolerant of yourself. You may want to be Superman or Superwoman, but this is not always possible.
- Embrace the learning opportunity inherent in all mistakes, but don't continue to make the same ones.

Action Steps

1. Consider how the contingent HR policies you have developed based on the discussion of Chapter 3 will support the recovery process. How flexible are they in meeting employees' needs and enabling them to return to work and heal simultaneously?

2. Put together a list of people you can call or count on to help you personally when a disaster strikes. You may want to consult people you know who have already gone through a disaster to ask them about their experiences, including what they would do differently the next time.

3. When you practice simulations as part of your business continuity plan, be sure to take into account how people may be expected to react.

Chapter 8

Building Resiliency While Helping Hearts and Minds to Heal

This chapter covers the following topics:

- Helping employees recover psychologically from trauma
- Professional support and counseling services available through the Employee Assistance Program and other avenues
- How managers and employees reacted to a real-life disaster, and how they used professional support to accelerate their recovery

Overview

Just as you can't predict when an emergency will hit, you can't calculate when it truly will have ended in the hearts and minds of your employees. Long after all physical evidence of a disaster is gone, people may still be suffering adverse effects from the experience. This is why flexibility in planning and in executing your plan is important; you need to acknowledge that disasters don't have neat and tidy endings. You may have to continue to provide expert support and counseling to help employees deal with the trauma and grief and continue on the road to recovery long after the event.

The discussion of emotions and conditions such as anger, weariness, depression, and post-traumatic stress disorder in this chapter is not meant to imply that everyone involved in a disaster will become one of the walking wounded for the rest of his or her working life. Individuals who have been employed for a significant portion of their lives tend to be highly functional human beings. They also tend to be resilient, which means that they are capable of both recovering from disaster and adjusting to change. Our goal is to shorten this period of recovery and adjustment by taking constructive steps.

Recent research confirms that a large number of individuals who experience trauma are indeed resilient.[1] Resilient individuals exhibit flexibility. They may experience some distressing emotions, but they promptly confront their challenges and engage in problem solving over the issues they face. Research also shows that brief workplace crisis interventions can positively affect the psychological well-being of individuals who have experienced a disaster. For example, New Yorkers who participated in just two or three brief counseling sessions at work after the events of 9/11 faced less long-term risk and overall mental health impairment for up to two years after the disaster compared with those who did not receive counseling.[2]

Psychological Recovery

Leaders should keep in mind the following three guidelines when helping employees to recover psychologically from trauma:

- Everyone with some connection to the situation, whether at the site of the event or at a different site, should have access to professional support and counseling services as soon as the danger of physical harm from the event is past. People may think they are fine, and they may be, but they may have a delayed reaction. The offer of support should extend to workers' families, who may be just as affected or even more so by the disaster.

    The HR staff at a firm based on the West Coast initially thought they had avoided the trauma of 9/11. Although their company suffered some financial loss because they had a partial ownership interest in the World Trade Center, their reaction was "Those were just buildings." A few days later, they learned that one of their two New York–area employees had been visiting the towers that morning and was now missing. Upon hearing about the fate of the employee, HR leaders took the initiative and contacted their EAP, which dispatched counselors to company work sites around the country to help employees come to grips with their loss.

- Support and counseling services should be tailored to the individual's situation; one size does not fit all. Generally, the people who personally experienced the incident will have the greatest interest in and need for support and counseling services.

For example, the fire in the First Interstate tower, which was described in the Prologue, was a much more disturbing experience for the employees who worked in the building or elsewhere in Los Angeles than for those in other cities. However, past experience may influence how individuals react, regardless of their physical proximity to the recent event. Those who have had prior traumatic experiences may have special needs.

The very gesture by the company of offering services is enough to start some employees on the road to healing. Others may resist using services, despite their emotional wounds, until they can find the precise sort of help that will serve as a salve for them. Still others will respond well to a number of different interventions, often provided over several months.

- Support and counseling services should remain available for at least a year, and possibly longer, because the healing process can be protracted. It's not uncommon for people who have been through a major trauma to experience relapses when they encounter situations or places that revive the painful memories. For example, an individual who "jumped back on the horse" and chose to ride the elevator after a fire in the office high-rise may suddenly start taking the stairs or request a transfer to a one-story building.

In your plans and actions, always keep in mind that the speed at which people recover, restabilize, and resume their lives can vary dramatically, depending on their proximity to the disaster, degree of involvement, prior experience with disasters, tolerance for stress, self-awareness and self-control, physical and psychological well-being, coping skills, and resiliency, as well as the actual and perceived helpfulness of others and a multitude of other factors, including the risks involved.

More on Employee Assistance Programs

Throughout this book we have suggested the utilization of Employee Assistance Programs, which usually provide crisis support. Since the 1950s these programs have evolved to become free-standing entities, available through contracts with HMOs, managed behavioral health firms, and insurance companies. A few EAPs function as company-operated crisis and counseling resources, although this situation is becoming increasingly rare.

An EAP can provide confidential, short-term counseling and referrals for employees and often for dependents and retirees as well. The counseling services may range from personal life adjustment sessions to workshops that target such common issues as balancing work and family life and handling interpersonal relationships in the workplace. In work-related disasters, most EAPs can provide trained counselors to conduct "critical incident stress debriefings," as well as to facilitate group discussions, meet with affected individuals one on one, hold workshops on living with sadness or stress, or provide other types of interventions. It

---

Publicizing EAP Services and Other Support Programs

To ensure that employees and their families know about EAP services and any other support programs that are available, communicate information about them regularly, especially in places where family members are exposed to the information. For instance, print and mail postcards to the home, insert reminders on pay statements, post flyers and posters at the work site, and include an announcement in all benefits updates. Be sure to feature the EAP in any special websites that go live after a crisis.

In addition to alerting employees and their families that the services exist, you need to explain how to use them. Also, specify who is eligible, especially if the services are available to extended family members.

For the first year after the disaster, consider monthly reminders. Don't worry about being repetitive. When stressed, people often can't absorb new information easily. Or if people don't think the information is immediately useful to them, they'll ignore it.

---

is important to be knowledgeable on the types of crisis services a particular EAP claims to supply.

By providing crisis support within 24 hours or sooner, an EAP can help affected employees and their families to realize that others share their reaction to stress, and to identify stressful situations and defuse them when possible. The EAP can also make referrals to other professionals if an individual needs more help or therapy.

If the EAP is your first line of defense, familiarize yourself with its capabilities, especially the services it offers and recommends and the qualifications of the counselors dispatched for your account. Make sure the EAP has the ability to send in specialized counselors on short notice (generally 24 to 48 hours), from their own staff or through partnerships with expert consultants in all of your locations.

Ask whether the EAP routinely provides follow-up services to help those most at risk. These services can range from coping skills, individual support through the EAP, mental health benefits, and community resources.

For instance, Magellan Health Services, a U.S.-based behavioral health disease management and employee assistance company, has developed a "Critical Incident Severity Index Scale" to assess the significance of traumatic workplace events. The higher the score on a number of factors, the greater the risk of negative impact on employees at the workplace.

For those incidents with a moderate to severe risk, Magellan suggests that employers adopt a three-phase extended follow-up for managers and employees. The first phase starts one or two days after the initiation of on-site services, which occurs shortly after the critical incident. The second phase is about a month later. The third takes place about 8 weeks later. In the case of severe incidents, such as the hurricanes of 2005, some organizations had a phase 4 follow-up about 12 weeks later. The follow-up can involve telephone consultations, group briefings, individual sessions, or other interventions that are appropriate for the situation, organization, and individuals. After each phase, Magellan captures information about the extent to which employees are functioning and approaching their pre-incident state. These extended services not only help affected individuals, but also demonstrate the employer's commitment to its employees.

Also, the EAP should be able to coordinate well with your internal security department, external health services, police, and your HR function. Once you know your EAP's strengths and deficiencies, plan how you will supplement its services in the face of a disaster or major risk.

One national expert in risk assessment and trauma counseling is Stephen White, President of Work Trauma Services, Inc. Dr. White has extensive experience helping people cope with crises, and he often provides backup or specialized services to EAP counselors. When an organization is faced with a damaging event of large

---

If an EAP Is Not Available

If your organization doesn't have an EAP, you have several options available to you, including the following ones, in order from the most extensive range of services to the least.

- You can contract with a local or regional EAP to provide in-person services on a fee-for-service basis at the time of the disaster. Telephone counseling services also may be available for a fee. The Employee Assistance Professional Association (EAPA) maintains a list of EAP providers on its website, http://www.eapassn.org.

- You can band with other employers in your geographic area as a local collaborative and secure a contract with an EAP. In this way you may be able to hire an EAP offering more services at a more reasonable rate because of the volume of potential patients you will be providing.

- You can talk with local resources, such as your local American Red Cross chapter, your county or city mental health services department, and your Chamber of Commerce, to determine what counseling services they have available during a crisis.

In any of these situations, suggests Suzanne Gelber—who specializes in substance abuse, mental health, and chronic disease and has worked with many EAPs—you'll need to vet the organizations and individuals ahead of time. Dr. Gelber also recommends that they be licensed as mental health counselors with emergency certification or be affiliated with CEAP (Community Emergency Assistance Program) and have emergency certification.

---

scope, services such as his, coupled with what the EAP provides, can be enormously valuable. From the employer's perspective, the sevices pay off not only by helping employees to stabilize more quickly, but also by preventing higher costs and more serious problems down the road. For example, a business that does not address employees' emotional and psychological problems can experience higher costs from medical claims, more absenteeism, higher turnover, and lower productivity over the next several years.

Disaster Packs

Consider providing disaster packs for employees, especially if your organization doesn't have an EAP.

Disaster packs are self-contained packages (such as manila envelopes) kept at the work site that individuals can open when a disaster strikes. The contents include action-oriented information, such as:

- Suggested actions to take in response to the incident that just happened (e.g., a bank robbery)
- Checklists of whom to call for help and others to notify
- Tips on dealing with immediate stress
- Phone numbers of community resources that can provide counseling help
- Other suggestions and checklists that may be helpful

According to Toni McClure, Chief Clinical Officer for Magellan Health's Midwest Care Management Center, these packages can be very helpful to employees, especially if the contents include a mix of information specific to the employer and guidelines on how to deal with the trauma.

Of course, these packs are helpful only if you prepare them in advance and make sure that employees know how to access them when a disaster occurs.

Three Stages of Disaster Recovery

Dr. White assisted First Interstate HR leaders and employees who had worked in the building that burned. He worked with the staff to educate them on dealing with the anger and weariness brought on by the situation and other, associated symptoms.

"These phenomena can be seen in other trauma-inducing incidents. Each case, though, is unique in terms of the nature of the stressor event, the various feelings manifested, and the severity of impact," he explained.

In First Interstate's experience, the affected staff went through three stages:

- *Stage 1: Reaction.* Hit with the reality of a disaster and immediate losses, people react with shock, disbelief, sadness, anger, and confusion. They search for information, share news and reactions with co-workers, and become preoccupied with the event. They may also experience sleep and appetite disturbances, excitedness, and fatigue and may ruminate about "what if." They have concern for and identify with other victims and worry about their ongoing safety.

- *Stage 2: Adjustment.* After a time the initial excitement subsides and the overall reality sinks in, especially after people have assessed their losses. They begin to mobilize and initiate recovery efforts. They may display mood swings, still subject to the range of reactions they experienced when the disaster occurred. They are probably frustrated by a lack of control over their situation and by the enormous challenges they face in dealing with lost resources. They may also feel hurt and resentful over a perceived lack of sensitivity from outsiders. They immerse themselves in their work and yet want more time and space to deal with the event, and they are constantly fatigued.

- *Stage 3: Restabilization.* Ultimately, individuals become more stable but experience occasional "echoes." Problems remaining from the disaster are finally overcome, changes are accepted as permanent, and conversation and attention turn to other events.

Anger and Weariness

When individuals experience great loss, their feelings can quickly transform to anger, according to Dr. White. This anger stems from numerous sources, including the need to:

- Endure the pain of losses
- Maintain work performance standards in spite of disruptions

- Sacrifice personal time in order to get matters of life and work under control
- Tolerate undesirable working conditions, such as crowding, loss of privacy, and constant interruptions
- Be a "host" or tolerate guilt as a host
- Depend on hosts for accommodations, resulting in a loss of self-reliance
- Deal with actual or perceived limitations (self-blame) that allow restoration accommodations to be distributed to others first
- Tolerate not having the answers to various questions and concerns

This anger is compounded by weariness that results from the drama and trauma in the days immediately following an emergency or a disaster. People will either show the anger directly or mask it with some other behavior. It's important to defuse anger and combat weariness so that employees can return to productive work without experiencing long-term adverse effects.

According to Dr. White, HR leaders and other managers should watch out for these negative adaptive behaviors:

- *Withdrawing from the recovery effort or withdrawing from work.* The employee is not participating in the tasks assigned to his or her unit or has left the workplace, and he or she is checking neither voicemail nor e-mail and is not carrying out assignments.
- *Keeping silent or showing hostility.* This may include such behaviors as being snippy, throwing temper tantrums, exhibiting a "Don't talk to me right now" attitude, putting down others, or using unnecessary sarcasm.
- *Demanding lots of special attention or treatment.* Suddenly, the employee is showing a need for high maintenance and reassurance.
- *Complaining.* The employee expresses the sentiment that nothing is any good or that he or she is being put upon unnecessarily.
- *Blaming.* It is someone else's fault that the work isn't getting done on time or with the quality expected.

- *Blowing up.* A normally cool and collected employee loses his or her temper and screams at others.
- *Curtailing generosity.* A normally benevolent, sharing person becomes selfish and seemingly uncaring about others.

Leaders and managers should also watch themselves and other managers for these problem behaviors:

- Emotional withdrawal from employees
- Deflecting voiced concerns
- Too much absorption in work versus concern for and involvement with staff
- Taking frustrations out on subordinates by making unrealistic work demands

Dr. White suggests that leaders and managers take these steps to deal with anger and weariness symptoms observed in themselves or in others:

- Be aware of the anger/weariness dynamic.
- Acknowledge to yourself and others that the reaction is normal and understandable.
- Encourage expressions of anger/weariness, including venting, to surface in a safe setting, as long as you and those involved agree on what this safe context is. For example, be explicit about honoring each other's confidentiality. Also, you may want to meet off-site, or at least in a room that's not a fishbowl.
- Share personal frustrations with subordinates and clients, as long as it's a safe setting.
- Listen and respond to legitimate grievances whenever possible.
- Focus on recovery efforts and practical problem solving.
- Confront persistently negative employees, such as foot draggers, sandbaggers, pouters, complainers, "yes but"-ers, and destructive cynics.
- Encourage physical exercise, which releases muscular tension.
- Encourage and create opportunities for competitive sports.
- Share good news about improvements, restoration, and successes as soon as possible.

- Emphasize and encourage personal replenishment activities and rituals.
- Make sure you are promoting the EAP benefit, especially to those who show greater-than-average difficulty in coping with the work environment and/or personal issues.
- Take advantage of opportunities for laughter, which eases burdens, counters hostility and depression, and promotes optimism.
- Accept that in extreme circumstances people need a little more nurturance, such as listening and caring.

Symptoms of Depression and Post-Traumatic Stress Disorder

According to the National Institute of Mental Health,[3] you need to be on the alert for the following symptoms:

- For *depression*: a combination of symptoms that interfere with the ability to work, study, sleep, eat, and enjoy once pleasurable activities, including feelings of hopelessness and pessimism; feelings of guilt, worthlessness, and helplessness; loss of interest or pleasure in hobbies and activities that were previously enjoyable, including sex; decreased energy, fatigue, being "slowed down"; difficulty concentrating, remembering, and making decisions; insomnia, premature awakening, or oversleeping; appetite and/or weight loss, or overeating and weight gain; thoughts of death or suicide, or suicide attempts; restlessness and irritability; and persistent physical symptoms that do not respond to treatment, such as headaches, digestive disorders, and chronic pain.

- For *post-traumatic stress disorder* (PTSD): nightmares; flashbacks; numbing of emotions; depression; feeling angry, irritable, or distracted; and being easily startled. Family members of victims can also develop this disorder. Most people with PTSD try to avoid any reminders or thoughts of the ordeal. PTSD is diagnosed when symptoms last longer than one month.

Because each situation is special, individuals are unique, and the resources available can vary widely based on your geographic location, you should plan to get professional help to address psychological problems immediately after a disaster, including screening for the degree of impact. This way you can be sure that bodies, hearts, and minds are coping adequately or are in the process of healing, and that people can begin to resume their lives.

Any major crisis can be a life-changing event. When we are shaken physically, mentally, and emotionally, we lose a little more of our innocence and we have to recalibrate our sense of what's normal. We will never be able to recapture our former state, but with effort we can create a new state of healthy normalcy.

Action Steps

1. Look into your EAP's services, and if they are inadequate for dealing with the effects of a disaster—such as insufficient breadth and depth of counselors in locations where you have employees—interview specialists from firms that can supplement your EAP during a crisis.
2. If you don't have an EAP, explore options immediately for providing professional support and counseling services, including employee screening after a disaster.
3. Provide employees with communication that describes the support and counseling services available to them and their families.

Chapter 9

Starting to Prepare Now—Five-Minute Planning Steps

This chapter suggests a number of planning actions that can each be carried out in five minutes. The basic idea is that some disaster planning is better than none, and the planning process need not be an onerous obligation.

Overview

For many of us, time is our most precious resource. Why spend it planning for events that might not occur when you already have many pressing demands? The answer is that a variety of unexpected things can happen, as the real-life examples in this book show, and those who took the time to plan generally have benefited from a faster, more complete recovery.

If you remain unconvinced that planning is worth your time, consider the following sets of actions that you can do in five-minute time slots. You may not solve all of the problems that arise, but you'll bring to the surface important issues that you can then handle one by one over time. By taking action in small bursts, you may be able to stay a few steps ahead when a disaster strikes. Carry out these actions in any order you choose—just take five to survive.

Connect with Your Internal Partners

When was the last time you checked in with your partners in disaster preparedness? Think about taking a few minutes to connect with individuals in the following departments:

- Safety and security
- Media in cities where employees are concentrated
- EAP
- Information technology
- Communications, including the individuals designated to make website/intranet changes quickly and to set up a special site
- Operations
- HR, including generalists in the field

Ask them what's new in their area in terms of disaster preparedness/ business continuity planning. Are they anticipating any changes? Have they attended any seminars of interest on this topic, or read any articles or books that might influence planning? Are their key messages up to date? Would there be any value in getting together in advance of the next simulation?

Refresh Records

Establish a regular schedule for updating key records, such as:

- Employee emergency contact information, including a local contact and an out-of-area contact
- Media lists
- Fact sheets for your company, facilities, and products
- Location of key data and supplies
- Posters, wallet cards, ID cards, website postings, and other materials that provide employees with directions on what to do in an emergency

Run Through Redundancies

How much redundancy have you built into your communications, so that if one method or system goes down, you can access alternative means? For example, you should allow for at least two, and preferably three or more, ways to:

- Reach key individuals using the e-mail addresses and phone numbers you have on record
- Send electronic and text messages
- Make phone calls, such as using cell, satellite, and landline phones. You should also have an old-fashioned analog phone at work and at home that you can use when the power is out

- Get the word out to employees
- Contact customers

Have you tested your multiple methods recently? Is there at least one backup person (and preferably two) to help you update your website/intranet or launch a special site?

Estimate Risk and ROI

If you're having difficulty getting your leaders' attention and help in preparing for a disaster and developing a business continuity plan, step back and perform the following analysis. (This exercise will take more than five minutes, but you can break it into steps.) You can either do a back-of-an-envelope calculation or something more sophisticated. Consider:

- Your organization's tolerance for risk. In general, the bigger the organization, the greater its ability to absorb losses and, therefore, the higher its tolerance for risk. But also take into account your organization's view toward insurance and other risks. And calculate how much business you'd lose if you had to shut down for several days, or even several weeks.

- The probability of a disaster. If you have no clue, make it 50%. Experts say that if you don't know, it's always best to assign equal probabilities.[1] (But if you're in southern Florida or on the Gulf Coast, make it closer to 100%.)

- The cost of disaster planning and business continuity planning, in both soft and hard dollars. As a rule of thumb, expect each member of the core team to put in 160 to 200 hours—about one month's work time. Estimate a half month for the other team members. Then think about hiring experts to help you. Also consider the hard-dollar cost of the supplies and services you'll need for handling the emergency and getting the business going again. (For more on this topic, see Chapter 2.)

- The return on investment (ROI). What if you could restart the business in two days instead of five? What would the difference in dollars be, less the one-time cost for disaster planning/business preparedness? How would this quick recovery help your reputation with customers, employees, investors, and other key groups?

If you want to get fancy, you also can consider the time value of money; you might ask individuals in your finance department for help with this. By carrying out any level of analysis, however, you can start to understand the value of disaster planning and preparedness.

Hunt and Tame the Silent, Sugarcoated Moose®

Do you face challenges from the Silent, Sugarcoated Moose regarding disaster planning? The Silent, Sugarcoated Moose is a mutated species of the "moose on the table" or the "elephant in the room." Everyone sees and knows about the moose, but no one says anything. And everyone continues to ignore it when someone tries to put a positive spin on negative news. Or people attempt to silence the moose, which feeds the rumor mill.

You can improve the situation by asking tough questions and practicing scenario playing, especially if your colleagues are dragging their feet or doing a sloppy job in their planning efforts. For example, you can ask your colleagues:

- What assumptions are we operating under as we're doing (or not doing) our planning? Are they still valid?
- What do you think our competitors or harshest critics would say or do if they knew we weren't taking disaster planning seriously, or were doing it haphazardly or carelessly?
- How would it look if our disaster planning problems were featured on the front page of the *Wall Street Journal* or the local newspaper?
- Are we thinking as creatively as possible in considering crises that could occur?
- Are there any potential crises smoldering within our organization that we're ignoring?
- Do our actions or decisions reflect the way we want to be remembered?
- What are the ramifications if we do nothing?
- What if there's no disaster? Can we still benefit from doing disaster planning and addressing the issues that have surfaced?

By confronting issues up close rather than tiptoeing around them, you can move people to take positive action.

Chew over Separation Anxiety

What dog trainers call "sep-anx" is a daily but surmountable challenge for their four-legged charges. When a disaster separates family members from each other and from their pets for long periods of time, anxiety on both sides escalates. If a significant number of your employees work in areas involving long commutes and heavy traffic jams, have you considered how they could be reunited quickly and safely with their family and pets under a variety of scenarios?

What support would you be willing to provide if it meant that employees could return to work faster? Or does it better fit your company culture to raise this issue in your emergency reminders and encourage employees to figure out the best alternative for them and their families?

Review with New Eyes

How about asking someone who has recently moved to the area to vet your business continuity plan? Their fresh perspective may uncover some vulnerability in your plan that deserves investigation. For instance, when Joe Bagan of Adelphia Communications moved from Denver to Florida in summer 2004 to become Senior Vice President of the Southeast Region, he noticed displays in Florida grocery stores that he had never seen in Colorado: suggested supplies to have on hand when a hurricane hits.

Bagan picked up a free guide on hurricane preparation and brought it to work. His senior leadership team reviewed the region's disaster preparedness plan against the guide and made some updates. He then asked each of the cable systems in the region to update their plans. Within a few weeks hurricane season was in full fury, and all the Adelphia cable systems in the Southeast were successfully putting their revised plans into action.

Check Your Supplies

What if the power were to go out in your office? Would you be able to do these basic activities (followed by recommended supplies in each case)?

- See (flashlight and candles)
- Make a phone call (cell phone or regular phone, preferably on an analog phone line)

- Listen to the radio (battery-operated radio)
- Watch TV (battery-operated TV)
- Send an e-mail or text message (cell or smart phone or wireless PC)
- Power your cell phone or PDA (car or hand-powered charger)

Would you have cash on hand? Would you have enough gas in your vehicle to be able to drive? If you think you or others might be caught flat-footed, stock up on supplies.

Build a "Just-in-Case" Inventory of Emergency Supplies

With many companies adopting "just-in-time" business practices in recent years to cut storage costs and ensure that inventory is fresh when it's needed, it can be difficult for consumers (businesses and individuals) to buy what they need when typical hiccups occur in the system, not to mention power outages, road closures, and other problems associated with disasters. Even if you and your organization are proponents of just-in-time inventory for your business supplies, you should consider adopting a *just-in-case* supply of emergency provisions for your work sites. Having supplies on hand is important for two key reasons: (1) you need easy access to them when a disaster strikes, and (2) you might not be able to get supplies, especially reasonably priced ones, when you need them.

You should also encourage employees to keep some emergency supplies at their homes and in their cars. See "Suggested Actions to Take at Home" in the Resources section on page 157.

What emergency supplies do you need? Experts say you should stockpile water, food, first-aid supplies, clothing, bedding, tools, and special items for common medical conditions. Both the Red Cross and the Occupational Safety and Health Administration (OSHA), as well as other organizations, have lists of recommended items on their websites. You also need to take into account the type of disaster that you are likely to encounter. For example, if you're in tornado alley or an area subject to hurricanes, the appropriate supplies may be slightly different from those needed for earthquakes.

These lists can change, especially information on how to rotate items to make sure the ingredients don't expire. You should consult the websites listed in the Resources section of this book starting on page 138.

Figure Out How to Make Your Small Size Work to Your Benefit

If you're a small employer, you may not have all the resources that larger companies have at their disposal for disaster and business continuity planning. Rather than use your size as an excuse for not doing all the necessary planning, reframe the issue. Think about how you can creatively partner with customers, employees, vendors, and other businesses to successfully confront a disaster and strengthen your business.

Ask yourself these questions:

- If the business takes a hit and has to halt operations for a few hours, days, or weeks, who will suffer, besides employees? Vendors, suppliers, customers, or others? Can you present a convincing business case for them to work together with you in disaster planning? Can you pool resources with them to respond to a disaster? If you don't have the cash to cover resources, could you barter time and your products or services?

- Are there businesses in your geographic area that you can join forces with? For example, can you and another company jointly hire experts and other resources, such as an EAP provider?

- If you're a member of the local Chamber of Commerce, Rotary Club, or other community-based business organization, do you know what services they provide to their members?

- Are you storing computer records, files, and other critical information off-site? Or are you using "on-demand" software or "software as a service," which allows you to run programs over the Internet so that you can access critical data wherever you are (assuming the Internet is up and you can access it)?

- Are there businesses outside your geographic area, even competitors, that you can approach about being a "disaster buddy"? You can help each other out by providing phone coverage, office space, customer support, and other services.

- Can you incorporate in audit plans the need to revisit the status of your business continuity planning?
- Do you know what your peers are doing in terms of the planning effort? Can you share ideas or combine resources with them?

Build Goodwill with Employees

Will your employees want to return to work after a disaster? Or will the disaster serve as a great excuse for them to leave and never return?

Now is the time to make an honest assessment of how employees rank you as an employer. To what extent do your employees view your organization as a good place to work? What data do you have to support your opinion? Have you done an employee survey lately? If so, what have you learned and what actions have you taken to make improvements? If not, it's probably time to check in with employees on a variety of issues, and also to assess the amount of goodwill you've accumulated.

Think about any changes you could make that would serve a dual purpose—both improving your reserve of goodwill and better positioning you to handle the people side of any disaster.

Action Steps

1. Decide where to begin planning, now that you've reached the end of the last chapter. Determine where you can get the most traction from your efforts. Also think about what interests and excites you most, and the area where you have the most energy. You may want to start there.
2. Talk to others who should work with you on the planning, and determine how you will work together. As you've seen throughout this book, disaster planning and business continuity planning are a team endeavor.
3. Get ready to lead people and make a difference!

Resources

In this section you'll find:

- A listing of resources to aid you in your research and planning efforts, leadership, and professional development
- An outline of the points to cover as you begin work on your business continuity plan
- A sample telephone tree
- A sample wallet card
- Employee emergency response procedures
- Suggested actions to take at home

Literature and Websites

For additional information, please visit this book's website: www.leadingpeoplethroughdisasters.com

Business Continuity Planning

Check out www.disasterrecoveryworld.com for a comprehensive resource on business continuity planning, with links to other websites. They offer the Business Continuity Plan (BCP) Generator, which is software that provides an efficient approach to developing a plan.

Be sure and get a copy of the Federal Emergency Management Agency booklet at www.fema.gov.

General Crisis Management

Albrecht, Steve. *Crisis Management for Corporate Self-Defense*. New York: Amacom, 1996.

This guide is "an arsenal of self-defense tools that will help you handle any crisis with minimal damage."

Barnes, James C. *A Guide to Business Continuity Planning*. New York: John Wiley & Sons, 2001.

General information on planning

Caponigro, Jeffrey. *The Crisis Counselor: A Step-by-Step Guide to Managing a Business Crisis*. Chicago: Contemporary Books, 2000.

Emergency Management Guide for Business and Industry
FEMA contract EMW-90-C-3348

Emergency Preparedness: Disaster Planning & Recovery: The Basics. SHRM Information Center, White Paper No. 61855, 1996.

Flett, Marsha. *Disaster Preparedness for Business.*
An extensive bibliography of books and articles related to helping businesses prepare for disasters. Available at http://mceer. buffalo.edu/InfoService/bibs/bibmay96.asp

Freestone, Julie, and Raab, Rudi. *Disaster Preparedness: Simple Steps for Business.* Menlo Park, CA: Crisp Publications, 1998.
This book provides easy-to-apply information about setting up a disaster action plan and disaster response teams, and getting employees involved in disaster preparedness.

Fullmer, Kenneth L. *Business Continuity Planning: Step-by-Step Guide with Planning Forms on CD-Rom.* Brookfield, CT: Rothstein Associates, 2000.

Harvard Business Review on Crisis Management. Boston: Harvard Business School Press, 2000.
A collection of eight essays, originally published in the *Harvard Business Review*, relating to how to deal with difficult situations, crises, and other sensitive topics in a business environment.

Kessler, Steven. "Damage Control." *Small Business Reports* vol. 17, no. 11, p. 16 (November 1, 1992).
Provides information on dealing with the aftermath of a crisis or disaster.

Lockwood, Nancy R. "Crisis Management in Today's Business Environment: HR's Strategic Role," *SHRM Research Quarterly* (2005).
Provides a summary of crisis management and the role HR practitioners can play.

Meyers, Kenneth N. *Manager's Guide to Contingency Planning for Disasters: Protecting Vital Facilities.* New York: John Wiley & Sons, 1999.
This book covers disaster planning with an emphasis on facilities.

Mitroff, Ian I. *Why Some Companies Emerge Stronger and Better from a Crisis: 7 Essential Lessons for Surviving Disasters.* New York: AMA-COM, 2005.
This book outlines what organizations need to do not only to survive a crisis, but also to become stronger and more confident through the experience.

Open for Business: A Disaster Planning Toolkit for the Small Business Owner. Institute for Business and Home Safety, 1999.

A how-to guide to developing a business continuity plan.

Reiss, Claire Lee. *Risk Management for Small Business*. Fairfax, VA: Public Entity Risk Institute, 2004.

Detailed checklists and analytical tools for assessing a variety of risks, including human and behavioral.

Tiogo, Jan William, and Tiogo, Margaret Romano. *Disaster Recovery Planning: Strategies for Protecting Critical Information Assets*. New York: Prentice-Hall, 1999.

Includes disaster planning with an emphasis on information management.

Wahle, Thomas, and Beatty, Gregg. *Detailed Planning Guide for Emergency Planning*.

Available at www.fema.gov.

Dealing with the Human Aspect of Trauma and Grief

Rivenbark, Leigh. "Recovering from Covering Carnage," *HR Magazine* vol. 45, no. 12, pp. 40–42 (December 2000).

While employees at Denver television station KUSA covered the Columbine High School shootings, HR Manager Alison Munn improvised a quick response to the stresses of covering the emotional news and coordinated everything.

Check out the booklets and program offered by Pritchett. Their booklets on coping with organizational change may be helpful to employees and managers facing troubled times. Available at www.pritchettnet.com.

Get a copy of the Federal Emergency Management Agency's booklet *Preparing for Disaster*. It's a very handy guide on what to do at home to prepare for a disaster. Call FEMA at 1-800-480-2520 or write to FEMA, P.O. Box 2102, Jessup, MD, 20794-2012.

Dealing with Natural Disasters

Leonard, Bill. "Fighting Fire with Teamwork," *HR Magazine* vol. 45, no. 12, pp. 46–48 (December 2000).

When a raging wildfire closed the Los Alamos National Laboratory at the same moment that 1,200 student employees were arriving for work, the lab's student program team had to overcome difficult conditions to deal with protecting human life and the business.

Lucilio, Jonathan, and Davis, Tim. "Expecting the Unexpected with Disaster Recovery Planning," *National Productivity Review* vol. 18, no. 4, pp. 11–16 (Autumn 1999).

This article, which describes the impact of a flood on the vault operations of a midwestern bank, illustrates the value of disaster recovery planning (DRP) in responding rationally and decisively to unforeseen, hazardous events. Application of the methods and procedures of DRP can avert the panic and major losses that often result when disaster strikes.

Employee Assistance/Behavioral Health Management

For detailed information about Employee Assistance Association programs and services, check out www.eapassn.org

Behavioral Health Management
  A magazine devoted to behavioral health issues. Check out www.behavioral.net.

For links to a variety of mental health resources, check out www.behavenet.com.

Leadership

Boyatzis, Richard E., and McKee, Annie. *Resonant Leadership: Renewing Yourself and Connecting to Others through Mindfulness, Hope and Compassion*. Boston: Harvard Business School Press, 2005.

Brockbank, W., and Ulrich, D. *Competencies for the New HR*. Ann Arbor: University of Michigan Business School, Society for Human Resources Management and Global Consulting Alliance, 2003.

Goleman, D., Boyatzis, Richard E, and McKee, A. *Primal Leadership: Realizing the Power of Emotional Intelligence*. Boston: Harvard Business School Press, 2002.

RBL Group. An *On-Line Human Resources Assessment; On-Line Intangibles Audit*.

> Available at www.rbl.net.

Sartain, Libby, and Finney, Martha I. *HR from the Heart: Inspiring Stories and Strategies for Building the People Side of Great Business*. New York: AMACOM, 2003.

Society for Human Resource Management.

> Competency information available at www.shrm.org/comptencies.

Susskind, Lawrence, and Field, Patrick. *Dealing with an Angry Public: The Mutual Gains Approach to Resolving Disputes*. New York: Free Press, 1996.

The book analyzes case studies of how public and private organizations handled extreme public opposition to policy changes or budget priority shifts. It outlines a method employed by numerous executives, known as the mutual gains approach to dispute resolution, to prevent escalating conflict and violence.

Ulrich, Dave. *Human Resource Champions*. Boston: Harvard Business School Press, 1997.

Ulrich, Dave, and Brockbank, Wayne. *The HR Value Proposition*. Boston: Harvard Business School Press, 2005.

Ulrich, Dave and Smallwood, Norm. *Why the Bottom Line ISN'T! How to Build Value through People and Organization*. New York: John Wiley & Sons, 2003.

University of Michigan. *Strategic Human Resource Development Program*.

> Available at www.execed.bus.umich.edu. Click on "Centers of Excellence."

Strategic Planning

Bradford, Robert W., Duncan, Peter W., and Tarcy, Brian. *Simplified Strategic Planning: A No-Nonsense Guide for Busy People Who Want Results Fast!* Westborough, MA: Chandler House Press, 1999.

Napier, Rod, Sidle, Clint, and Sanaghan, Patrick. *High Impact Tools and Activities for Strategic Planning: Creative Techniques for Facilitating Your Organization's Planning Process.* New York: McGraw-Hill, 1998.

Strategic planning software and white papers can be found at www.planware.org/index.html.

Internet Resources

Academy of Organizational and Occupational Psychiatrists: www.aoop.org

American Academy of Experts in Traumatic Stress: www.aaets.org

American Management Association: www.amanet.org

Association of Contingency Planners International: www.acp-international.com/drba

Business Continuity Institute: www.thebci.org
Checklists and handouts that can be downloaded are available at this site.

Business Recovery Managers Association: www.brma.com
Provides useful links to organizations related to business recovery.

Charles Pizzo's crisis communication website, www.charlespizzo.com/hurricane
Includes communication lessons learned from Hurricane Katrina.

Centers for Disease Control and Prevention: www.cdc.gov

Common Symptoms after a Critical Incident: www.ucsc.edu/currents/terrorist_crisis/critical_incident_stress/

Contingency Planning and Management: www.contingencyplanning.com
Membership association offering free subscription to magazine and useful links.

Dealing with Loss: www.counselingforloss.com

Disaster Plan.com: www.disasterplan.com
This site includes the Disaster Recovery Yellow Pages, a comprehensive listing of product and service providers.

Disaster Preparedness and Response: http://palimpsest.stanford.edu/bytopic/disasters/

Disaster Preparedness for People with Disabilities: www.jik.com/disaster.html

Disaster Recovery Journal: www.drj.com
To access articles, use the password: world)

Disaster Recovery Shop: www.disaster-recovery-plan.com

Disaster-Resource.com: www.disaster-resource.com

Food and Drug Administration: www.cfsan.fda.gov

Grief Recovery Online for All Bereaved: www.groww.com

Institute for Business and Home Safety: www.ibhs.org

International Critical Incident Stress Foundation: www.icisf.org/CIS.html

Management Assistance Program: www.mapnp.org/library/
Provides an extensive collection of basic how-to management information to managers and supervisors, including information on dealing with disasters.

MIT's Business Continuity Plan: http://web.mit.edu/security/www/pubplan.htm

Provides an excellent prototype for a business continuity plan.

National Emergency Management Association: http://nemaweb.media3.net/index.cfm

National Fire Protection Association: www.nfpalearn.org

National Institute for the Prevention of Workplace Violence: http://workplaceviolence911.com

Contains model policies and a self-audit.

National Safety Council: www.nsc.org

Occupational Safety and Health Administration (OSHA): www.osha.gov/SLTC/smallbusiness/sec10.html

Red Cross: www.redcross.org/pubs

Rothstein Associates: www.rothstein.com

Has a catalog on disaster recovery planning and a wide-ranging list of books, articles, and newsletters on emergency preparedness/business continuity planning.

Small Business Administration: www.sba.gov

Society for Human Resource Management (SHRM): www.shrm.org

Trak-It-Down: www.trak-it-down.com

Has connections and links to places, persons, products, and services relating to HR.

United Behavioral Health: www.unitedbehavioralhealth.com

A provider of behavioral health services as well as an information center.

U.S. Department of Homeland Security: www.ready.gov

Their website has excellent references for emergency planning and business continuity planning.

Your Doorway to Disaster Recovery: www.yourdoorway.to/disaster-recovery

An open portal.

An Outline for Business Continuity Planning

This outline is intended to help you begin to develop your own business continuity plan. The outline is excerpted from the Federal Emergency Management Agency (FEMA) booklet *Emergency Management Guide for Business & Industry* and sample plan documents.

You can use this outline to jump-start your planning process. However, we strongly recommend that you also get a copy of the FEMA booklet. It has detailed information about each of the steps identified here and also identifies substeps. You can purchase it or download it from www.fema.gov/library/bizindst.pdf.

1. Planning steps
   a. Step 1: Establish a planning team
      i. Form the team
      ii. Establish authority
      iii. Create and issue a plan mission statement
      iv. Establish a schedule and budget
   b. Step 2: Analyze capabilities and hazards
      i. Review internal plans and policies
      ii. Meet with outside groups
      iii. Identify codes and regulations
      iv. Identify critical products, services, and operations
      v. Identify internal resources and capabilities
      vi. Identify external resources
      vii. Do an insurance review
      viii. Conduct a vulnerability analysis
      ix. List potential emergencies

         x. Estimate probability
       xi. Assess the potential human impact
      xii. Assess the potential property impact
     xiii. Assess the potential business impact
     xiv. Assess internal and external resources

c. Step 3: Develop the plan
       i. Write an executive summary
      ii. Describe emergency management elements
    iii. Describe emergency response procedures
    iv. Add support documents
     v. Detail the development process
    vi. Identify challenges and prioritize activities
   vii. Write the plan
  viii. Establish a training schedule
    ix. Continue to coordinate with outside organizations
     x. Maintain contact with other corporate offices
    xi. Review the plan, conduct training, and revise the plan
   xii. Seek final approval
  xiii. Distribute the plan

d. Step 4: Implement the plan
       i. Integrate the plan into company operations
      ii. Conduct employee training
    iii. Determine the planning considerations
    iv. Evaluate training activities
     v. Evaluate employee training
    vi. Evaluate and modify the plan

2. Disaster management issues to consider

a. Direction and control
       i. Emergency Management Group (EMG)
      ii. Incident Commander
    iii. Emergency Operations Center (EOC)
    iv. Security isolation of the incident scene
     v. Coordination of outside response

b. Communications
       i. Contingency planning
      ii. Emergency communications
    iii. Methods of communication

  (1) Employee and family communications
  (2) Notification
  (3) Warning
 c. Life safety
   i. Evacuation planning
   ii. Evacuation routes and exits
   iii. Assembly areas and accountability
   iv. Shelter
   v. Training and information
   vi. Family preparedness
 d. Property protection
   i. Planning considerations
   ii. Protection systems
   iii. Facility shutdown
   iv. Records preservation

3. Community outreach
 a. Community involvement
 b. Community service
 c. Public information
 d. Media relations

4. Recovery and restoration
 a. Planning considerations
 b. Continuity of management
 c. Employee support
 d. Resuming operations

5. Administration and logistics
 a. Administrative actions

6. Processes to think about
 a. Evacuation plans
 b. Communication plans
 c. Building security
 d. Reconstruction of computer services
 e. Restoration of accounting services
 f. Reconstruction of files
 g. Mail handling
 h. Employee relations
 i. Stress reduction

A Sample Telephone Tree

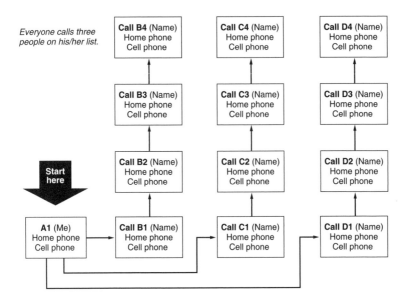

Everyone calls three people on his/her list.

Call B4 (Name)
Home phone
Cell phone

Call C4 (Name)
Home phone
Cell phone

Call D4 (Name)
Home phone
Cell phone

Call B3 (Name)
Home phone
Cell phone

Call C3 (Name)
Home phone
Cell phone

Call D3 (Name)
Home phone
Cell phone

Call B2 (Name)
Home phone
Cell phone

Call C2 (Name)
Home phone
Cell phone

Call D2 (Name)
Home phone
Cell phone

Start here

A1 (Me)
Home phone
Cell phone

Call B1 (Name)
Home phone
Cell phone

Call C1 (Name)
Home phone
Cell phone

Call D1 (Name)
Home phone
Cell phone

A Sample Wallet Card

 Organization Name
Employee Emergency Hotline
1-800-XXX-XXXX after a major disaster

- Take safety precautions
- Turn on AM/FM radio or TV
- Try and contact your supervisor
- Go to http://www.xxxxxxxxxxx for updates also

Where to Report

Report to your assigned shelter at ——————— if so instructed on the hotline.

Your temporary work location is at ———————— and you may be instructed to report there when you call the hotline.

Special Attention

Call the cool line at 1-800-XXX-XXXX if you want to talk to someone about the crisis or get updates on the situation.

Employee Emergency Response Procedures

Earthquake

These procedures are excerpted from the University of California at Santa Barbara Department of Emergency Operations procedures.

Outside

- Get to an open area away from trees, buildings, and power lines.

In a Vehicle

- Pull to the side of the road away from underpasses, bridges, and buildings.
- Remain in the vehicle until the shaking stops.
- Do not leave the vehicle if a power line has fallen on or near it.

Inside

- Stay away from windows, and get under a desk or a table.
- Duck, cover, and hold.
- In a hallway, sit against the wall and protect your head with your arms.
- In an auditorium, duck between the rows of seats and protect your head.
- Wait inside until the shaking stops, then evacuate the building and go to your emergency assembly point.
- Do not use elevators for evacuation.

- Designated personnel should assist individuals with mobility disabilities to reach a safe location—that is, an enclosed stairwell landing with a ground-level exit to the exterior or, if that is obstructed, inside an office separated from the hallway by a door.
- Do not reenter the building until you have been authorized to do so by emergency response personnel.

Preventing Fires

Careless management of work and storage areas and of electrical equipment is a common factor in office fires. Stockrooms and vault storage areas, for instance, should be kept uncluttered to prevent fires.

- Do not block aisles or exits.
- Maintain supplies and files in a neat and orderly manner. Periodically inspect areas for fire safety.
- In an area that is not protected by a sprinkler system, **do not** store materials closer than 36 inches from the ceiling.
- In an area that is protected by a sprinkler-system, **do not** store materials closer than 18 inches from the sprinkler heads.
- **Do not** smoke in storage areas. Remember that smoking on the premises is illegal in the city/state of _____

Keep work areas free of excess paper. A concentrated collection of papers and files on desks and filing cabinets makes excellent fuel. Before leaving at night, eliminate that unnecessary fire hazard by placing as many papers and files as possible in closed drawers or file cabinets.

Overloaded electrical outlets are the cause of many building fires. **Do not** create an octopus by inserting a series of two-way or three-way plugs into the same outlet. Connect only **one** cord to each receptacle socket. The use of extension cords is prohibited. If you need additional outlets, contact the Maintenance Department. When plugging or unplugging electrical equipment, be sure it is turned **off**; avoid touching metal or standing on a wet surface when doing so. For your safety, unplug electrical equipment by holding the plug and pulling it out of the socket; do not pull on the cord.

An office machine or appliance—such as a coffeemaker, calculator, or photocopier—carelessly left on could overheat, burn out, and ignite a fire. Whenever you leave your immediate work area, take a quick look around to be sure that all of your machines are set to the **off** position. The last person leaving the area at night should also take time to double-check that all machines are **off**. (This does *not* include computer equipment.)

Watch for electrical equipment that doesn't appear to be working properly or that is giving off an unusual odor. Report any strange odors from appliances or lights to your supervisor, as this could be the first indication of a fire.

When a Fire Occurs

If you are present when a fire starts, there are several basic safety rules to remember that could save your life.

- *Remain calm.* Your own common sense is the finest safety device ever developed. **Walk**—do not run—to the nearest exit.

- *Prepare yourself in advance.* Know where to go and how to get there. Heavy smoke often obscures exit signs. If you count how many doors you must pass on your evacuation route to reach the nearest exit, then, should you encounter heavy smoke, you can crawl or crouch low and count the doors as you make it to safety.

- *Establish an alternative route* in the event your first route is blocked or unsafe to use.

- *Before opening an exit door, touch the top and bottom of the door lightly with your hand.* If it is **hot,** do not open it. If it is not hot, open the door slowly. Stand behind the door and to one side, and be prepared to close it quickly if fire is present.

- *Follow the instructions of fire department personnel* and other officials handling the situation.

Whom to Call

If you discover a fire, notify the fire department *immediately.* Don't delay! Don't assume that someone else has called. Don't be embarrassed if the fire is a small one, perhaps just in a wastepaper basket. Remember, most large fires begin as small ones. The first five minutes are often more important in fighting a fire than the next five hours.

The Fire Department **must** be called whenever a fire occurs—even a small trash fire that was put out immediately by employees. The department will dispatch personnel to make a report. This report is necessary for several reasons, including insurance. (After the fire, forward a copy to the Security Department and Emergency Planning Unit.)

Whenever a fire occurs, the facility or building manager should immediately notify the Emergency Planning Director, Fire and Safety Unit, and Security Department by telephone.

What to Say

Be prepared to report to the fire department the following information:

- Nature of the emergency
- Exact address and cross street
- Telephone number from which you are calling (in a highrise, give your security console number or the building manager's number)
- Your name
- Floor number
- Area or department

Note: Do **not** hang up first; additional information may be needed from you.

Emergency Telephone Numbers

The following telephone numbers should be placed on every telephone facility in your building.

- Fire Department   911
- Emergency Medical Service   911
- Police Department   911
- Federal Bureau of Investigation   _____
- Security Department   _____

Evacuation Procedures

The safety of employees and customers is the overriding consideration. Preservation of company assets, records, and premises is important, but materials and property should not be protected at the risk of jeopardizing the safety of employees or the public.

The decision to evacuate is made by the senior managers who are responsible for determining the course of action to be taken during an emergency; it is based on information provided to them by key personnel at the emergency site. Fire or police department personnel may also order an evacuation.

If there is no fire in your area, but the alarm has sounded, wait at your primary exit until you have been notified to evacuate.

When evacuating:
- Remove high heels to avoid tripping.
- Walk, do **not** run.
- Do **not** push or crowd.
- Use handrails.
- Proceed to your evacuation point unless otherwise instructed.

If you relocate outside the building:
- Move away from the building quickly.
- Watch for falling glass and other debris.
- Stay with your floor warden.
- Do not talk to the press. If they ask questions, refer them to the Incident Commander or other managers in the emergency chain of command.
- Do **not** return to the building until you are notified that it's safe to do so.

If you become surrounded by smoke before you can evacuate:
- Drop to your hands and knees, keeping your face as close to the floor as possible. Because smoke rises, the air will be cooler and cleaner near the floor.
- If you have a handkerchief or scarf, cover your face. Hold your breath as much as possible; otherwise, breathe through your nose as shallowly as possible.

If you are forced to advance through flames:
- Hold your breath; move quickly and, if possible, cover your head and hair with a jacket, shirt, or similar material. Keep your head down and your eyes closed as much as possible.
- If you become trapped, call the Fire Department and the building manager for assistance. If possible, seek refuge in a room that is not burning or filled with smoke. Stuff the

cracks around the door with whatever cloth you can find. If possible, wet the cloth with whatever water is available—from a flower vase, drinking fountain, or even a coffee pot.

- If you are in a room with a window that can be opened, open it slightly at the top and bottom. The space at the top will exhaust smoke and the space at the bottom will admit outside air.

- If the room starts to fill with smoke and the windows cannot be opened, wait before breaking a window until you absolutely must (to stay conscious). Once a window is broken, smoke and gases can enter the room from outside.

If your clothing catches fire:

- Stop, drop to the ground, and roll.

Fire Extinguishers

The general rule is: **Never** attempt to fight a fire alone. **Always** use the buddy system. If someone must put a fire extinguisher into operation, do not just stand by and watch. Quickly find another extinguisher and return to the fire, then stand by. If the first extinguisher empties before the fire is completely out, you will be prepared to finish the job.

The basic rules for using an extinguisher are referred to as the three P's: Pull—Point—Press.

- **Pull** the pin while holding the extinguisher upright.
- **Point** the extinguisher at base of the flames.
- **Press** down the handle and fan across the flames from side to side.

Never place a used extinguisher back in its cabinet; it must be recharged to ensure its future effectiveness. One more caveat: If you are not trapped, and the fire is rapidly spreading, it is time for you to retreat! In this case, the fire should be left to trained professionals. Don't try to be a hero!

Sheltering in Place

Sometimes there is no choice but to stay inside a building until a conflagration such as a forest fire blows over. If you are ever advised to "shelter in place":

- Isolate yourself as much as possible from the external environment.
- Shut down air-handling systems.
- Shut all doors and windows and seal the cracks around them with tape or whatever you can find.
- Remove flammable materials such as curtains from the window area and move fabric-covered furniture to the center of the room.
- Provide for your own comfort.
- Communicate your needs to fire personnel.
- Notify emergency management personnel of your status.
- Monitor all available communications.
- Notify your family as soon as possible of your delayed arrival.

Severe Weather

Any kind of severe weather can have an impact on business and your safety. Adhere to the following guidelines.

At home:

- Assess conditions prior to leaving home.
- Listen to all available media for conditions, as well as news releases from the company on the designated FM station.
- Call the assigned emergency number to determine whether the company has been closed.
- Do not risk your life in order to return to work.

At work:

- Call the extension number provided to find out if the company has been closed.
- Listen to media reports, especially those on the company's designated FM station.
- Check your e-mail for pertinent messages.
- If the Emergency Operation Center (EOC) has been activated, contact your department safety representative (DSR) for any pertinent information and instructions on emergency procedures. The DSR will complete a department status report and transmit it to the EOC.
- Do not leave and use the roads if you have not been able to verify that it is safe to do so.

Hazardous Materials

Follow this checklist for **major** incidents involving a release of a hazardous material (chemical, biological, radiological, asbestos, etc.) that cannot be controlled by department personnel.

- Alert personnel from affected and adjacent areas.
- If possible, use signs and/or barricades to isolate the area.
- Evacuate the area and close the door.
- If the release cannot be contained in the area, activate the nearest fire alarm.
- Call **911** and explain what has happened.
- Stay upwind of the building.
- Ask for assistance from your department emergency response team member (if applicable).
- Do not reenter the building until you have been authorized to do so by emergency response personnel.

Utilities

The following procedures apply to utility emergencies.

Natural Gas

- If you smell gas, call **911** and evacuate to your emergency assembly point.
- Do not turn on electrical equipment or light switches.

Electrical

- Unplug sensitive equipment not connected to a surge protector.
- Disconnect hazardous equipment according to the department plan.
- After a power outage, check elevators for trapped individuals and call **911**.
- Stay away from downed power lines.
- During an extended power outage, you may have to leave the building and go to an emergency assembly point, where you will wait for further instructions from emergency response personnel.

Water

- Do not drink from any water system after an earthquake or a flood.

Bomb Threats

All bomb threats should be considered authentic until fully investigated.

To promote consistent, safe, and thorough practices in response to bomb threats or other matters relating to explosive devices, the following procedures should be followed.

- The person receiving the bomb threat should remain calm and attempt to obtain as much information as possible from the caller (see the checklist that follows).
- Call **911** to inform the Police Department of the situation.
- The police will *assist in determining* if an evacuation is necessary.
- Inform your supervisor and/or department head.
- If you spot a suspicious object or package, report it to the police; under no circumstances should you touch it.
- If instructed to evacuate, move to your department's emergency assembly point (EAP) *provided it is at least 300 feet from the building.*
- It is possible for radio transmissions to detonate certain devices, so do not transmit radio signals or use cellular phones within 300 feet of the targeted area.
- Do not reenter the area until you have been authorized to do so by emergency response personnel.

The Police Department *may* post the following sign at the entrance:

WARNING

XYZ organization has received an anonymous bomb threat against this building. We have no way of knowing if this is a serious threat. Officials have conducted a preliminary search and have found no suspicious items. Whether or not you enter is a matter of your personal discretion. —Management

---

Bomb Threat Checklist

Questions to ask the caller:
- When is the bomb going to explode?
- Where is the bomb?
- What does the bomb look like?
- What kind of bomb is it?
- What will cause the bomb to explode?
- What is your name?
- Where do you live?

Caller description:

Sex _____   Age _____   Race _____

Caller's voice:

Calm	Loud	Stutter
Angry	Laughing	Lisp
Excited	Crying	Deep
Slow	Nasal	Distinct
Raspy	Normal	Soft
Ragged	Rapid	Slurred
Distinguished	Accent	Familiar

Background sounds:

Street noise	Voices	Clear
Music	Animals	Static

Report the call immediately by dialing 911.

Emergency Evacuation Procedures
Individuals with Mobility Problems

Emergency procedures require that everyone exit a building when the fire alarm is activated. If you are an individual with a mobility-related disability and you are situated on the ground floor of a building, you should follow evacuation procedures according to the department plan. However, safety regulations require that elevators not be used for fire or earthquake evacuation because they may be damaged and unreliable. During emergencies when an elevator is not available for use, the following procedures apply to evacuations in multistory buildings for those unable to use the stairs.

When the fire alarm is activated, designated personnel should assist/escort individuals with mobility disabilities to a safe location (an enclosed stairwell landing that leads to an exterior exit at ground level). Someone should remain with the individual while another person notifies arriving emergency personnel of the location of anyone who needs assistance. The instructions of the safety personnel should be followed, and in no case should an attempt be made to move the individual to another building level, unless there is imminent danger in the safe refuge (e.g., heavy smoke in the stairwell).

An individual working alone who is unable to utilize the stairs should call 911 and report the planned refuge location (stairwell landing). Anyone unable to reach a stairwell (e.g., due to smoke) should close all doors into the area, call 911, and wait for emergency personnel to arrive.

Suggested Actions to Take at Home

This material is excerpted from the booklet *Preparing for Disaster*, published by the Federal Emergency Management Agency. Order it at 1-800-480-2520.

For Your Home

A. Get informed.

    1. Check with local agencies such as the Red Cross or community disaster planning agencies to gain an understanding of community resources.

    2. Make a family plan.

        a. All family members should know what to do, where to go, and whom to call in case of an emergency.

        b. Decide on an out-of-town contact that all family members can call; this can be family central.

        c. Have a family communication plan in writing, and make sure everyone has a copy.

        d. Identify escape routes and safe places.

        e. Plan for your pets.

        f. Plan for those with special needs.

        g. Prepare for different types of emergencies.

B. Adopt this action list.

    1. Determine what to do about your utilities.

    2. Get a fire extinguisher and keep it charged.

    3. Check on your insurance coverage.

    4. Take Red Cross first-aid and CPR courses.

    5. Take an inventory of your home possessions.

6. Safeguard important family documents.
7. Minimize your home hazards.
C. Assemble disaster supplies kit at home.
   1. Water: Have one gallon of water per person per day on hand, and keep at least three days' worth.
   2. Food
      a. Ready-to-eat canned meats, vegetables, fruits, juices, milk and soup
      b. Staples for cooking—sugar, salt, and pepper
      c. High-energy foods such as peanut butter, jelly, crackers, granola bars, and trail mix
      d. Vitamins
      e. Formula or food for infants and for people on special diets
      f. Comfort/stress foods: cookies, hard candy, cereal, lollipops, instant coffee, and tea bags
   3. Pet supplies: Food, blankets, leashes, chew toys
   4. First-aid supplies
      a. Assorted bandages and gauze pads
      b. Cleaning agent/soap
      c. Hypoallergenic adhesive tape and latex gloves
      d. Assorted sizes of safety pins, tweezers, and scissors
      e. Needle, antiseptic, thermometer, and tongue blades
      f. Moistened towelettes and petroleum jelly
   5. Clothing and bedding
      a. Sturdy shoes, rain gear, sunglasses, hat and gloves, warm coats, thermal underwear, and other winter gear if you live in a cold climate
      b. Blankets or sleeping bags
   6. Tools and emergency supplies
      a. Paper cups and plates, and plastic utensils
      b. Flashlight and radio, with extra batteries for each
      c. Utility knife, can opener, pliers, compass, and map
      d. Fire extinguisher and shut-off wrench to turn off household gas and water
      e. Plastic sheeting, tube tent, aluminum foil, duct tape, plastic containers, matches, paper and pencil
      f. Plastic garbage bags with ties, a bucket with a tight lid, household chlorine bleach, and disinfectant

7. Special items
   a. Baby supplies, such as bottles and diapers
   b. Necessary medications or medicines, extra eyeglasses/contacts, dentures, and other special supplies
   c. Important family and financial documents in a waterproof, portable container
8. Maintain your plan.
   a. Review every six months.
   b. Run drills.
   c. Restock outdated food supplies.
   d. Test your fire extinguisher.

D. In case of a disaster:
   1. If instructed to take shelter, do so at once.
   2. If instructed to evacuate, know what to do and where to go.
   3. After the disaster, follow instructions.
   4. Know what to do if power is lost.

In Your Car

1. Flashlight, extra batteries, and maps
2. First-aid kit and manual
3. White distress flag
4. Tire repair kit, jumper cables, pump, and flares
5. Bottled water and non-perishable foods (e.g., granola bars)
6. Seasonal supplies
   a. Winter: blanket, hat, mittens, shovel, tire chains, windshield scraper, fluorescent distress flag
   b. Summer: sunscreen lotion, shade umbrella, hat or visor
7. Sturdy shoes

Notes

Foreword

1. Shawn Fegley and Justina Victor, *2005 Disaster Preparedness Survey Report*, Society for Human Resource Management, Alexandria, VA, October 2005.

The Purpose of This Book

1. Libby Sartain and Martha I. Finney, *HR from the Heart: Inspiring Stories and Strategies for Building the People Side of Great Business*, AMACOM, New York, 2003.

Prologue

1. Shawn Fegley and Justina Victor, *2005 Disaster Preparedness Survey Report*, Society for Human Resource Management, Alexandria, VA, October 2005.

2. Lillian Gorman and Kathryn D. McKee, "Disaster and its Aftermath," *HR Magazine*, 35(3), 54–58, March 1990.

Chapter 1

1. James M. Kouzes and Barry Z. Posner, *The Leadership Challenge*, 3rd ed., Jossey-Bass, San Francisco, 2002.

2. Dr. Boyatzis worked with Dr. David McClelland both at Harvard and at McBer & Co. on the initial work that gave rise to the field of competency assessment and development. Dr. Boyatzis's seminal book, *The Competent Manager: A Model for Effective Performance*, published in 1982, set the stage for much of the work that followed.

3. Richard E. Boyatzis, Diana Bilimoria, Lindsey Godwin, Margaret Hopkins, and Tony Lingham, article to appear in Yuval Neria, Raz Gross, Randall Marshall and Ezra Susser, eds., *9/11: Mental Health in the Wake of Terrorist Attacks*, Cambridge University Press, New York, 2006.

Chapter 8

1. George A. Bonanno, "Loss, Trauma and Human Resilience," *American Psychologist*, 59(1), 20–28, January 2004.

2. Joseph A. Boscarino, Richard E. Adams, and Charles R. Figley, "A Prospective Cohort Study of the Effectiveness of Employer-Sponsored Crisis Interventions after a Major Disaster," *International Journal of Emergency Mental Health*, 7(1), 9–22, Winter 2005.

3. National Institute of Mental Health, http://www.nimh.nih.gov.

Chapter 9

1. David R. Henderson and Charles L. Hooper, *Making Great Decisions in Business and Life*, Chicago Park Press, Chicago Park, CA, 2006.

Acknowledgments

Many people donated their time and expertise in telling us their stories and passing on the important lessons they learned under challenging circumstances. We appreciate their reliving their experiences to contribute to this book. We also are grateful for the number of national and international experts who talked with us about their work in the context of the human side of crises, including crisis leadership.

In particular, we want to acknowledge the following people. We thank William Nickey and Kathleen McComber, SPHR, for sharing their horrific experiences that are mentioned in the book, along with Chuck Nielsen, Retired EVP HR, from Texas Instruments; Mike Rogers, SPHR, BancFirst; Sue Tempero, SPHR, retired, from the *Des Moines Register*; Lynda Brown, SPHR, PhD, and John Valvo, SVP HR, retired, from Standard Chartered Bank. Among their experiences are the sudden death of a CEO, the Oklahoma City bombing, the Des Moines flood, working through intense corporate challenges, and the 9/11 destruction of the World Trade Center.

We also thank Charles Pizzo, crisis communications consultant and past Chairman of the Board of IABC (International Association of Business Communicators), and Gerard Braud of Gerard Braud Communications, who specializes in media training, crisis management, video production, and professional speaking, for sharing their personal experiences of Hurricane Katrina from the perspective of native New Orleanians as well as crisis communications experts.

We appreciate the insights from the 2004–2005 hurricane seasons provided Joe Bagan, Senior Vice President of the Southeast Region of Adelphia Communications, and Ray Dravesky, Director of Employee Communications, also of Adelphia. Michael Hissam, Regional Director, Communications of Delphi's Mexico operations, shared his experiences in dealing with employees and the media after a 1985 tornado, and in dealing with border crossings between Mexico and the United States on 9/11. Margery E. Zylich APR, Assistant Vice President, Operational Communications and Special Projects for MedStar Health, shared her experiences with the 1998 shooting at Washington Hospital Center's Cancer Institute, including her award-winning crisis communications. Tish Kelly-Mick, Manager of News Services in Corporate Communications of Agilent Technologies, Inc., offered samples of employee communications that Agilent provided after the 2004 tsunami and the 9/11 attack.

Special thanks to Richard E. Boyatzis, PhD, Wayne Brockbank, PhD, Tom Lawson, PhD and Stephen Schoonover, MD, for sharing their expertise on leadership and its competency frameworks; Mory Framer, PhD, for his insights in dealing with individual and large-scale trauma; Stephen G. White, PhD, for his contributions on workplace trauma; Mitch Marks, PhD, for sharing his knowledge of how leaders need to look out for and manage themselves during difficult periods; Suzanne Gelber, PhD, an expert policy consultant and researcher focused on substance abuse, mental health, and chronic disease and a partner of the Avisa Group, for sharing her knowledge and expertise of employee assistance programs and mental health; and Steve Shulman, Chairman and Chief Executive Officer of Magellan Health Services and several of his team members, including Rick Lee, President of Employer Solutions, David Wadell, General Manager of the Midwest Care Management Center, and Toni McClure, Chief Clinical Officer of Midwest Care Management Center, for sharing their expertise and experiences with critical incidents, especially their scoring method, which considers factors that influence an incident's potential impact on the workplace and the need for follow-up care.

Thanks to Larry Parsons of the University of California at Santa Barbara, who spent time with us discussing business continuity and emergency response and shared his plan documents; Roy Dugger of the American Red Cross, who ensured we covered all the bases; Jack Armstrong, veteran Incident Commander, who vetted the chapters on leadership and business continuity planning and who enlightened us on what it's like to be an Incident Commander; Jerry Roberts, Vice President of News and Editor of the *Santa Barbara News-Press*, who coached us on style and substance; and Marilyn

Weixel, SPHR, and Jenni-Marie Peterson, PHR, who helped with research and additional content.

Special thanks are due to Gayla Visalli for her consummate professionalism and skills in helping us turn rough copy into the pages we presented to Berrett-Koehler Publishers.

And a very special thank–you goes to Steve Piersanti and the entire team at Berrett-Koehler, for their care and dedication in coaching us through the editing and publishing process.

Kathy McKee gives hugs to Grant and Scott McKee for sharing her with this book, and she also gives all of her HR team members and colleagues at First Interstate Bank her continuing gratitude for their courage, commitment, and dedication during the trying times they all had to get through together. Special thanks are due to Lillian Gorman, former Executive Vice President of Human Resources of First Interstate Bancorp, for her vibrant leadership at the top during our many disasters. And Kathy gives very special recognition to her former colleagues at Standard Chartered Bank, who suffered through two attacks on the World Trade Center and kept going in spite of the adversity.

Liz Guthridge thanks her husband, David Matthews, for his love and devotion, and his patience with all of her special writing and consulting projects. She acknowledges Tomas and his cousin, Dharma, who both serve as therapy dogs. They have deepened her understanding and appreciation of the bonds between humans and animals, and the critical need for animal rescue as well as human rescue during disasters. She also wants to recognize all of her former New York City neighbors with whom she endured the 1989 Gramercy Park steam pipe explosion, the subsequent asbestos cleanup, and the rest of the aftermath.

Index

About the Authors

Kathryn McKee began her career in Human Resources at Mattel, Inc. in its early years, where she learned to thrive and survive in a fast-paced Human Resources/Industrial Relations environment. She then moved to Twentieth Century Fox Film Corp and helped create one of the first HR functions in the motion picture industry.

She moved next to First Interstate Bancorp as Senior Vice President of Compensation and Benefits. Kathryn then moved to First Interstate Bank Ltd., as the Chief HR officer of that division, and she then joined Standard Chartered Bank as Senior Vice President and Region Head of HR for the UK-based bank. She now is President of Human Resources Consortia, where she offers consulting on Human Resources strategy, leadership, and executive coaching.

Her leadership and governance background includes serving as 1991 Chairman of the Society for Human Resource Management; and President of the SHRM Foundation, the Human Resource Certification Institute, and the National Human Resources Association. She is listed in *Who's Who in America*. She was honored by NHRA as its 1986 Member of the Year; by PIHRA in 1990 with its Award of Excellence in Human Resources; by SHRM in 1994 with its Award for Professional Excellence; and by the Santa Barbara Human Resources Association in 2004 as its Member of the Year.

She loves to write, and her previous publications include the chapter "Moving as the Markets Move: Planning for Resizing," in *Resizing the Organization*; "Human Resources: Insurrection or Resurrection," published in the *Human Resource Management Journal*; and "New Compensation Strategies for Emerging Career Patterns" with Beverly Kaye, which was published by *HR Magazine* and won the distinguished William W. Winter Award from the American Compensation Association.

She graduated from the University of California at Santa Barbara and is a graduate of UCLA's Anderson School of Management Executive Program.

Liz Guthridge specializes in strategic employee and change communication. She is the founder of Connect Consulting Group LLC, based in the San Francisco Bay Area.

A results-oriented, seasoned consultant, Liz has more than 25 years of experience helping companies communicate more effectively with employees to build trust and achieve business goals. Liz excels in helping leaders to confirm, clarify, and communicate what they want to do and to build buy-in from key constituents.

Over the years, she has consulted with companies across a variety of industries facing a range of challenges, including bankruptcy and mergers and acquisitions.

In addition to her award-winning communication consulting for her clients, Liz frequently writes and speaks on communication and change topics. She also advises communication professionals on how to increase the capabilities and capacity of their communication functions.

Before starting Connect, Liz worked for several change management and HR consulting firms, including Mercer Delta, Towers Perrin, and Hewitt Associates. She also worked for Amoco (now BP) in public and government affairs and was a reporter for the *Huntington (W.Va.) Advertiser.*

Her first job was serving as the first female vendor for the Tulsa Oilers, the Triple A affiliates of the St. Louis Cardinals baseball team. As a crusading junior high investigative reporter she experienced firsthand as a vendor being the subject of media coverage. The job provided other excitement too. She still remembers listening to the organist play *Raindrops Keep Falling on My Head* as a tornado touched down a few miles from the ballpark.

She holds an MA in communication management from the University of Southern California, Annenberg School for Communication; an MBA from the University of Connecticut; and a BSJ in journalism from Northwestern University, Medill School of Journalism.

About Berrett-Koehler Publishers

Berrett-Koehler is an independent publisher dedicated to an ambitious mission: Creating a World that Works for All.

We believe that to truly create a better world, action is needed at all levels—individual, organizational, and societal. At the individual level, our publications help people align their lives with their values and with their aspirations for a better world. At the organizational level, our publications promote progressive leadership and management practices, socially responsible approaches to business, and humane and effective organizations. At the societal level, our publications advance social and economic justice, shared prosperity, sustainability, and new solutions to national and global issues.

A major theme of our publications is "Opening Up New Space." They challenge conventional thinking, introduce new ideas, and foster positive change. Their common quest is changing the underlying beliefs, mindsets, institutions, and structures that keep generating the same cycles of problems, no matter who our leaders are or what improvement programs we adopt.

We strive to practice what we preach—to operate our publishing company in line with the ideas in our books. At the core of our approach is *stewardship*, which we define as a deep sense of responsibility to administer the company for the benefit of all of our "stakeholder" groups: authors, customers, employees, investors, service providers, and the communities and environment around us.

We are grateful to the thousands of readers, authors, and other friends of the company who consider themselves to be part of the "BK Community." We hope that you, too, will join us in our mission.

Be Connected

Visit Our Website
Go to www.bkconnection.com to read exclusive previews and excerpts of new books, find detailed information on all Berrett-Koehler titles and authors, browse subject-area libraries of books, and get special discounts.

Subscribe to Our Free E-Newsletter
Be the first to hear about new publications, special discount offers, exclusive articles, news about bestsellers, and more! Get on the list for our free e-newsletter by going to www.bkconnection.com.

Participate in the Discussion
To see what others are saying about our books and post your own thoughts, check out our blogs at www.bkblogs.com.

Get Quantity Discounts
Berrett-Koehler books are available at quantity discounts for orders of ten or more copies. Please call us toll-free at (800) 929-2929 or email us at bkp.orders@aidcvt.com.

Host a Reading Group
For tips on how to form and carry on a book reading group in your workplace or community, see our website at www.bkconnection.com.

Join the BK Community
Thousands of readers of our books have become part of the "BK Community" by participating in events featuring our authors, reviewing draft manuscripts of forthcoming books, spreading the word about their favorite books, and supporting our publishing program in other ways. If you would like to join the BK Community, please contact us at bkcommunity@bkpub.com.